SHELLEY LEITH

MAKEOVER

PARTICIPANT'S GUIDE

ZONDERVAN.com/
AUTHORTRACKER
follow your favorite authors

ZONDERVAN

Head-to-Soul Makeover Participant's Guide: Helping Teen Girls Become Real in a Fake World

Requests for information should be addressed to:

Zondervan, *Grand Rapids, Michigan 49530*

ISBN 978-0-310-67042-1

Cover and interior design: SharpSeven Design

Printed in the United States of America

20 21 /DCI/ 23 22 21 20 19 18 17 16 15 14 13 12

CONTENTS

WHY DO I NEED A HEAD-TO-SOUL MAKEOVER?

What a fake world we live in. Fake tans. Fake eyelashes. Fake teeth. Fake hair. Fake smiles. In such a plastic society, where pretending is normal and faking it is admired, it is all-too rare to come across a person who is real and genuine. Such a person is a breath of fresh air to be around, and we are drawn to her because she doesn't act stuck-up, doesn't put on masks, and doesn't try to be someone she's not.

But for many of us, it's hard to be real. There are things about us we'd like to hide or change. Maybe that's why makeover shows are so popular on television right now. We watch in fascination as a person gets a new chin or a different hairstyle, a wardrobe overhaul or a forced exercise regimen. We imagine what it would be like to get a head-to-toe makeover...how much more confident we'd feel, how popular we'd be, how we could relax and not worry about what others are thinking of us. We'd *finally* be able to be real.

Well, every single one of us needs a makeover. Not a head-to-toe makeover, but a head-to-soul makeover. And in this study, that's what we're all going to get! We'll change what's bothering us in our *heads*—things like insecurity, anxiety, stress, irritability, and envy—by working on character qualities in our *souls*—such as confidence, courage, self-control, patience, and contentment. The more we develop these character qualities, the more like Jesus Christ we will be—and that's what it takes to be truly real in a fake world.

HOW THIS STUDY WORKS

TELEVISION REALITY SHOWS

This study uses a different television reality show each week to teach us about the character flaws we need to overcome. For example, we'll use the show *American Idol* to learn about pride, and *Fear Factor* to explore fear and anxiety.

SELF-ASSESSMENTS

You'll take a magazine-type self-assessment every week to discover where in your life you might have a particular character flaw. The "reveal," which is sometimes surprising, lets you know which aspect of the character flaw you should work on over the next week. If you want to know how your results compare with other participants, go online and do the self-assessments at www.headtosoulmakeover.com.

LEARNING ACTIVITY

There's a fun exercise in every lesson. Whether it's tossing an old habit in the trash can or building a house of cards with your group, each week includes a playful activity to help you discover and deepen a positive character quality.

BIBLE LESSON

The Bible is the original makeover manual. In it are lessons that can help us form our character and make us more like Jesus Christ. We'll spend time every week exploring a Bible passage or story and talking together about how it can help us become more real.

MAKEOVER CHALLENGE

At the end of each meeting, you get to choose a Makeover Challenge to try during the upcoming week. This is an action step that you'll work on to help you get stronger in a character quality and overcome a character flaw in your life.

MAKEOVER JOURNAL

You'll track your progress in your Makeover Journal. Week by week you will get to record what happens as you encounter different situations that give you a chance to practice your Makeover Challenge. You can also blog about your experiences at www.headtosoulmakeover.com.

MAKEOVER TEAM

You and two others will form a Makeover Team, which is your accountability group for the whole study. You'll be given personal things to discuss together and suggestions for encouraging one another throughout the week.

LET'S DO IT!

Unlike reality-show makeovers that wash off with the next shower or start looking shabby over time, your Head-to-Soul Makeover has eternal benefits. When you join forces with God to overcome the character flaws that have been messing you up, you'll discover that God has created you to be a person of power, confidence, and hope. And you know what else happens as a side-benefit of a Head-to-Soul Makeover? You will become more genuine and real—and that is the most attractive type of person to be around!

So, are you ready to get started on the best makeover ever? Then, in the words of the *Extreme Makeover: Home Edition* team, "LET'S DO IT!"

EPISODE 1

WHAT NOT TO BE

CHAT ABOUT IT...

In this study we're going to look at what it means to be *real* in a fake world. Each week, we're going to use a different *reality* television show to illustrate the character qualities that help us become more *real*.

If you could be on a reality show—which one would you choose and why? You can choose one of these—or some other one!

- *The Biggest Loser*—where people compete to lose the most weight
- *What Not to Wear*—where people are coached to transform their fashion disasters
- *Extreme Makeover*—where people are transformed by plastic surgery
- *Trading Spaces*—where friends redecorate each other's rooms
- *Extreme Makeover: Home Edition*—where a family receives a whole new house

WHAT NOT TO BE

Today's lesson is based on the reality show *What Not to Wear*, except we're renaming it *What Not to Be*. For our show, we'll be focusing on character rather than clothes.

Girls nominated for *our* show, *What Not to Be*, have character flaws that make them irritating or unattractive. The coaches have ten weeks to give these girls "head-to-soul makeovers" that will help them become better people.

If you had to describe a teenage girl to be on the show, *What Not to Be*, what kinds of negative character qualities would she have? (Note: We're not naming people we'd nominate for the show—instead we're talking about character traits that need to be tossed in the trash can.)

CHECK YOURSELF

Let's get personal now. For this episode you have nominated *yourself* to go on the show because you've noticed you keep having troubles with your parents, or in your relationships with your friends, or inside your head. You suspect you might have some character flaws, and you want to get help from a coach to become a more real and likeable person.

Let's begin this ten-week adventure by taking the *What Not to Be* Quiz. Taking the quiz is kind of like when the coaches on *What Not to Wear* go through a person's closet, identifying "fashion disaster" clothes. This will help you identify character flaws you need to throw in the garbage can—character qualities you should work on over the next ten weeks so that you can become more real.

Take the *What Not to Be Quiz* now. You can take it on the pages that follow, or online at www.headtosoulmakeover.com. (Be sure to print your results if you take the quiz online.)

WHAT NOT TO BE QUIZ

For the following three sets of character flaws, rate each flaw from 1 to 5.

1 = I never or almost never feel or act like this.

2 = I rarely feel or act like this.

3 = I sometimes feel or act like this.

4 = I often feel or act like this.

5 = I always or almost always feel or act like this.

SET 1

______ A. Self-centered
______ B. Insecure
______ C. Fearful
______ D. Obsessive
______ E. Impatient
______ F. Jealous
______ G. Hate interruptions
______ H. Difficulty finishing

SET 2

______ A. Judgmental
______ B. Low self-esteem
______ C. Anxious
______ D. Overly emotional
______ E. Intolerant
______ F. Rarely satisfied
______ G. Trouble sharing things
______ H. Easily discouraged

SET 3

______ A. Perfectionistic
______ B. Feel worthless
______ C. Untruthful
______ D. Stressed out
______ E. Demanding
______ F. Restless
______ G. Greedy
______ H. Avoid decisions

SCORE YOURSELF: Total your scores by adding up your 3 A's, your 3 B's, etc.

EXAMPLE: _3_ A. Self-centered + _4_ A. Judgmental + _2_ A. Perfectionistic = _9_ A's

REVEAL: *Circle your top 3 scores. These are 3* ***character flaws*** *that you need to throw in the garbage can, and the* ***character quality*** *that will help you overcome them and become more genuine.*

A's ________The character flaw of **Pride** is 'thrown away' by developing **Humility**.
B's ________The character flaw of **Insecurity** is 'thrown away' by developing **Confidence**.
C's ________The character flaw of **Fear** is 'thrown away' by developing **Courage**.
D's ________The character flaw of **Anger** is 'thrown away' by developing **Self-Control**.
E's ________The character flaw of **Impatience** is 'thrown away' by developing **Patience**.
F's ________The character flaw of **Envy** is 'thrown away' by developing **Contentment**.
G's ________The character flaw of **Greed** is 'thrown away' by developing **Generosity**.
H's ________The character flaw of **Quitting** is 'thrown away' by developing **Perseverance**.

TRY IT OUT

For this activity, your leader will be passing paper T-shirts out to the entire group. Choose one of your top three character flaws and write it on your paper T-shirt. Think about why that flaw was one of your top three, and take turns sharing your thoughts with the rest of the group. Then come forward and toss your paper shirt in the trash can and say which positive character quality you're going to work on to help you "throw away" that flaw and become more genuine.

TALK IT OVER

Just in case you're thinking *What Not to Be* is all about making you popular, let's talk a little bit about the Most Real Person Ever. On *What Not to Wear*, when the coaches want to show their guest how to dress well, they demonstrate sample outfits on a mannequin. For our *What Not to Be* show, we have a living model who shows us what it means to live out these character qualities—Jesus.

Now, Jesus wasn't always popular. Not everyone approved of him. In fact, he alienated some people. So, why are we calling him the Most Real Person Ever? Because he possessed character qualities that pleased God, which meant he was genuine. He did what was right and loved people.

Can you think of stories from the Bible where Jesus exhibits the character qualities that make a person genuine?

A person who is genuine, or real, doesn't always appeal to everyone. If you have the courage to do the right thing, some people may feel alienated. When you reach out and love certain people, they may run away. But a genuine person treats others in ways that are caring. She doesn't change who she is to try to gain the approval of others. Jesus wasn't concerned about being popular. He was concerned about pleasing God, and that is a mark of true character.

So, on our show, *What Not to Be*, the goal is to "throw away" our character flaws and replace them with qualities that make us look and act like Jesus. The Bible calls this *process* discipleship, and it calls the *end result* being Christlike.

A MAKEOVER TAKES WORK

Have you ever been part of a team—such as a sports team, a musical group, or a drama production? Share the kinds of drills your coach or director has you do during practices.

Have you ever noticed that you don't improve your skills simply by joining the team? You improve your skills by practicing the disciplines, repeating the basics, and rehearsing the techniques. The same is true with improving your character. A *Head-to-Soul Makeover* doesn't happen just because you join the "Christian team." Take a look at these words from the apostle Paul:

> ***Train yourself*** *to be godly. For physical training is of some value, but godliness has value for all things, holding promise for both the present life and the life to come.* (1 Timothy 4:7-8)

According to this verse, what can we do to ourselves to achieve godliness (which is another word for being like Christ)? How much value is there in becoming godly?

It is important to realize that godliness doesn't just happen. It is something we choose to work on and train into ourselves, which is what this *Head-to-Soul Makeover* is all about. Consider what Paul writes in Romans 5:3-4 (TLB):

> *We can rejoice, too, when we run into problems and trials, for we know that they are good for us; they help us learn to be patient. And patience develops strength of character in us and helps us trust God more each time we use it until finally our hope and faith are strong and steady.*

How is it that problems can make us rejoice? If strength of character makes us strong and steady, what does a life without strong character look like? Can you think of a time when you didn't trust God and it made the situation worse?

Think again about your experiences as part of a team. How does being part of a group that's working together toward a shared goal help you achieve more than you could alone?

FORM A MAKEOVER TEAM

We're now going to form Makeover Teams of three girls each. These teams will stay together for the next ten weeks. Once you are with your new team, ask one another this question: *What were your top three character qualities to work on—and why?* Send text messages, IMs, or emails to one another this week, offering encouragement and prayers to the other members of your team, such as "God, give Emily courage when she does her speech tomorrow." Be sure to exchange phone numbers, email addresses, and other contact info so you can connect during the week.

MY MAKEOVER TEAMMATES

(Name, phone number, email address, Facebook page, etc.)

WHAT NOT TO BE

MAKEOVER JOURNAL • WEEK 1

THIS WEEK'S MAKEOVER CHALLENGE

Start keeping your Makeover Journal. Begin your journal by listing the three character flaws you need to throw away and the related character qualities you need to work on. Throughout this week, record situations that come along that trigger one of the character flaws you ranked high on your quiz. (For instance: If fear is one of your flaws, and you're asked to give a speech in class that triggers fear in you, write that down!) Then look at the character quality that can help you deal with this problem (in this case, courage), and rejoice! God has given you a chance to practice this quality and make it stronger in your life!

Want to blog about it? Keep your Makeover Journal online at www.headtosoulmakeover.com.

MY TOP THREE CHARACTER FLAWS	THE CHARACTER QUALITIES I NEED
1. ______________________	______________________
2. ______________________	______________________
3. ______________________	______________________

DATE: ______________

WHAT WAS THE SITUATION? ______________________________

____

WHICH CHARACTER FLAW DID THIS SITUATION TRIGGER? ______________

____

HOW DID THE ASSOCIATED CHARACTER QUALITY HELP ME (OR NOT)?

____

____

DATE: ____________________

WHAT WAS THE SITUATION? ____________________

____

WHICH CHARACTER FLAW DID THIS SITUATION TRIGGER? ____________________

____

HOW DID THE ASSOCIATED CHARACTER QUALITY HELP ME (OR NOT)?

____

____

DATE: ____________________

WHAT WAS THE SITUATION? ____________________

____

WHICH CHARACTER FLAW DID THIS SITUATION TRIGGER? ____________________

____

HOW DID THE ASSOCIATED CHARACTER QUALITY HELP ME (OR NOT)?

____

____

DATE: ____________________

WHAT WAS THE SITUATION? ____________________

____

WHICH CHARACTER FLAW DID THIS SITUATION TRIGGER? ____________________

____

HOW DID THE ASSOCIATED CHARACTER QUALITY HELP ME (OR NOT)?

____

____

DATE: ____________________

WHAT WAS THE SITUATION? ____

____

WHICH CHARACTER FLAW DID THIS SITUATION TRIGGER? ________________

____

HOW DID THE ASSOCIATED CHARACTER QUALITY HELP ME (OR NOT)?

____

____

DATE: ____________________

WHAT WAS THE SITUATION? ____

____

WHICH CHARACTER FLAW DID THIS SITUATION TRIGGER? ________________

____

HOW DID THE ASSOCIATED CHARACTER QUALITY HELP ME (OR NOT)?

____

____

DATE: ____________________

WHAT WAS THE SITUATION? ____

____

WHICH CHARACTER FLAW DID THIS SITUATION TRIGGER? ________________

____

HOW DID THE ASSOCIATED CHARACTER QUALITY HELP ME (OR NOT)?

____

____

EPISODE 2

CHAT ABOUT IT

From your Makeover Journal, share something that happened this past week that gave you a chance to practice one of your character qualities.

This week, imagine yourself as a contestant in the singing competition reality show, *American Idol*. Thousands of hopefuls audition for this show, but many of the contestants are deluded about their musical abilities. Eventually, the field is narrowed to the top 12 performers, and telephone voting determines the "American Idol," who gets a recording contract and national fame.

Have you ever won a competition, election, or tryout? Did winning change you in any way? Can you think of any examples of people who were changed by fame or wealth or success?

FOUR PRIDEFUL IDOLS

There are four types of pride that we can see among contestants on *American Idol*. And we may see the same kinds of pride among people we meet—or even in our own lives. Do you recognize any of these kinds of people?

- **Idol 1 thinks too much of herself:** This contestant has limited talent, but claims everyone tells her she's a great singer.
- **Idol 2 thinks too little of herself:** When this contestant is complimented, she puts herself down: "You really thought that was good? I don't think I sang very well."
- **Idol 3 thinks too little of others:** This contestant criticizes the judges and other contestants.
- **Idol 4 ignores input from others:** This contestant thinks she always knows best. When contestants ignore the judges' advice because they think they know better, they usually find themselves voted off the show.

CHECK YOURSELF

Let's try out for our Character Makeover version of *American Idol,* called *Prideful Idol.* In this tryout you'll discover which of the four Prideful Idols you are.

Do the *Prideful Idol Tryout* now, either here or online at www.headtosoulmakeover.com.

TRYOUT

There are four types of pride seen in typical American Idol *contestants. Circle the number corresponding to how frequently you think you have exhibited each type of prideful attitude in the last few weeks.*

RARELY / ONCE IN A WHILE / SOMETIMES / FREQUENTLY

IDOL 1: I THINK TOO MUCH OF MYSELF

1 2 3 4 **Looking out for Number 1:** I seek to get the best for myself.

1 2 3 4 **Exaggerating:** I embellish the truth to make myself sound better.

1 2 3 4 **Name dropping:** Knowing important people makes me feel important.

1 2 3 4 **Self-centeredness:** I am insensitive to the needs of others. "It's all about me."

1 2 3 4 **Showing off:** I call attention to my possessions, abilities, or goodness.

IDOL 2: I THINK TOO LITTLE OF MYSELF

1 2 3 4 **False humility:** I point out my shortcomings, looking for reassurance.

1 2 3 4 **Undeserving:** I can't receive compliments, gifts, or help; I don't feel I deserve them.

1 2 3 4 **Overworking:** I do more than what is expected, looking for affirmation.

1 2 3 4 **Woe is me:** I often have some catastrophe I'm complaining about, looking for sympathy.

1 2 3 4 **Failure:** I feel I need to try hard because I haven't earned God's approval yet.

IDOL 3: I THINK TOO LITTLE OF OTHERS

1 2 3 4 **Argumentative:** When others speak, I focus on what I disagree with and argue about it.

1 2 3 4 **Critical:** I often find ways in which others don't meet my standards.

1 2 3 4 **Irritable:** I get annoyed easily and point out things that bother me.

1 2 3 4 **Judgmental:** I'm quick to assume the worst about people.

1 2 3 4 **Put-downs:** I intentionally belittle others with cutting or snubbing remarks.

IDOL 4: I IGNORE THE INPUT OF OTHERS

1 2 3 4 **Defensive:** If I'm caught in an error, I usually believe it wasn't my fault.

1 2 3 4 **Ignores suggestions:** I don't like to listen to advice. "You're not the boss of me."

1 2 3 4 **Isolated:** I reject help from others, preferring to go it alone.

1 2 3 4 **Refusal to change:** "This is just the way I am, so accept me."

1 2 3 4 **Unteachable:** I am closed to input or guidance. I have my act together.

TRYOUT RESULTS:

Idol 1: I Think Too Much of Myself	Total:	____________
Idol 2: I Think Too Little of Myself	Total:	____________
Idol 3: I Think Too Little of Others	Total:	____________
Idol 4: I Ignore the Input of Others	Total:	____________

TOTAL PRIDEFUL IDOL SCORE: ________________

SCORING:

1-20 *You are a model of genuine humility.*

21-40 *You are learning to be more and more humble. Way to go!*

41-60 *Thank you for your honesty. That's the first step to humility!*

61-80 *Hmm! You have some work to do.*

Now that you have done the *Prideful Idol Tryout*, which type of Prideful Idol did you find most surprising to have on the list? Which of the Prideful Idols are the most difficult for you to be around? Which Prideful Idol total was highest for you?

TALK IT OVER

THE *TRUE* AMERICAN IDOL

Let's turn our attention to the character quality that helps us be a true American Idol—not the kind you worship, or the kind who is prideful, but someone who is genuine and deeply attractive, a person people want to be around. **This quality is humility.** Now, you may be thinking humility is something it's not. Humility doesn't mean dressing ugly, letting everyone boss you around, or feeling worthless. Humility *does* mean **thinking rightly about who you are in relation to God.** Right thinking is realistic thinking—knowing your *real* strengths, your *true* weaknesses, your *genuine* talents, and your *real* worth. When you think *realistically* about yourself, you're "being a *real* person in a fake world"!

The scale below shows three kinds of thinking. On the right is boastful thinking, which is the most obvious form of pride. But, on the left end of the scale is false humility, the kind of thinking that says "everyone is better than me"—which is actually another form of pride. Such thinking is prideful because it's still all about getting people to focus on us, give us attention, and reassure us that we're not as pitiful as we say we are. Humility is balanced in the middle. Humility means you have a right view of who you are and who you're not, and who God is—and that you just ain't him! When your eyes are always on yourself and whether you're better—or worse—than others, that's pride. When your eyes are on God, you can't help but be humble.

EVERYONE'S BETTER THAN ME!	I HAVE A RIGHT VIEW OF WHO I AM IN RELATION TO GOD.	I'M BETTER THAN EVERYONE!
FALSE HUMILITY = PRIDE	**HUMILITY**	**BOASTFUL = PRIDE**

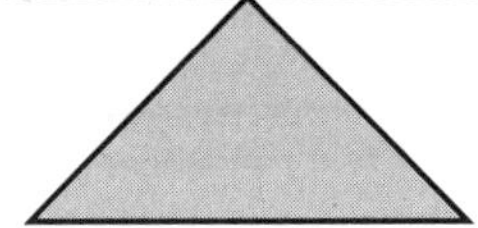

INTRODUCING OUR "HUMBLE IDOL"

Do you know who Jesus named as the greatest person ever born? Well, it wasn't Moses of Red Sea and Ten Commandments fame; it wasn't David, who was a "man after God's own heart"; it wasn't Abraham, the father of the nation of Israel. Rather, it was the scruffy, wild-eyed hermit, John the Baptist, about whom Jesus said, "I tell you the truth: Among those born of women there has not arisen anyone greater than John the Baptist" (Matthew 11:11). Now, why was John the Baptist Jesus' top pick for World's Greatest Guy? Because he was humble. Let's see what we can learn about humility from our Humble Idol, John the Baptist.

1. A humble person has the right perspective about who she is. She says, "God is God—and I am not." Consider what John the Baptist once said:

> *"After me will come one more powerful than I, the thongs of whose sandals I am not worthy to stoop down and untie."* (Mark 1:7)

How does this statement show that John the Baptist was humble? Why isn't this false humility? What could you say about how you compare to Jesus that would show the right perspective on who you are?

2. A humble person directs people's attention to God. She says, "It's not about me." Take a look at our next passage:

> *The next day John was there again with two of his disciples. When he saw Jesus passing by, he said, "Look! The Lamb of God!" When the two disciples heard him say this, they followed Jesus.* (John 1:35-37)

How does this scene from John's life show that he was humble? How do you think he felt when his disciples left him? What can you say in certain situations to point people away from you and toward God?

3. A humble person is not self-focused but God-focused. One problem with achieving humility is that it's impossible to develop it by working on it directly. The more you focus on humility, the more you are focusing on yourself, which is prideful. So how are you supposed to work on humility if working on it makes you prideful? Well, John the Baptist had a two-part formula:

> *"He must become greater, I must become less."*
> (John 3:30)

TRY IT OUT

THE MIRROR EXPERIMENT

Here's how this works. *(Mirrors and small paper squares will be passed out to the group.)* Look at your reflection in the mirror. Now, keep looking at yourself, but think about the **second part** of our formula for humility: *"I must become less."* So, try *not* to think about yourself right now... Is it possible?

Now, while looking in your mirror, we're going to try the **first part** of the formula: *He must become greater."* Put the paper in front of the mirror, then move it closer and closer to your eyes until you can no longer see your reflection.

- *What just happened? Describe what you saw in the mirror as the paper got closer to your eyes.*
- *So, when working on the quality of humility, what happens when you try to start with the second half of the formula: "I must become less"?*
- *At the moment the paper blocked out your reflection, were you thinking of yourself or the paper?*
- *So, what happens to your thoughts about yourself when you start with "He must become greater"?*
- *What are some ways you can increase how much you focus on God?*

CHECK IN WITH YOUR MAKEOVER TEAM

Go back to your *Prideful Idol Tryout* and share with your team which type of pride tends to be the biggest problem for you and why. In your Makeover Journal for this week, choose your Makeover Challenge; share with your team which one you chose and why. Arrange to contact one another this week to check in on how you're doing on your God Hunt and the challenge you chose for the week.

MAKEOVER JOURNAL WEEK 2

CHOOSE A MAKEOVER CHALLENGE

Choose a challenge based on what type of Prideful Idol you are, and write about how you do this week in your Makeover Journal. Want a daily reminder? Sign up at www.headtosoulmakeover.com.

If you scored highest in…	…try this Makeover Challenge to become more humble.
Idol 1. I think too much of myself.	☐ I will stop bragging, exaggerating, or showing off. I will do something nice for someone in secret, so I don't get noticed.
Idol 2. I think too little of myself.	☐ I will stop pointing out my shortcomings. I will practice simply saying "Thank you" when someone compliments me.
Idol 3. I think too little of others.	☐ I will stop being so judgmental. I will find something complimentary to say to a person whom I often find irritating.
Idol 4. I ignore the input of others.	☐ I will stop thinking I'm always right. I will say, "You're right, thank you for helping me," to someone who offers me advice.

MAKEOVER BONUS CHALLENGE: GO ON A GOD HUNT

To focus more on God and less on you, go on a God Hunt this week. Look for and then record in your Makeover Journal those moments when you see God show up in your day. Such times may include things you see in nature, interruptions, cool coincidences, delays, things that go right, frustrations, talks you have with people, answers to prayer—anytime you see signs of God's presence with you.

DATE: ______________________

Makeover Challenge

I tried my Makeover Challenge to become more humble, and here's what happened...

____

____

God Hunt

Today, I saw God show up when...

____

____

DATE: ______________________

Makeover Challenge

I tried my Makeover Challenge to become more humble, and here's what happened...

____

____

God Hunt

Today, I saw God show up when...

____

____

DATE: ______________________

Makeover Challenge

I tried my Makeover Challenge to become more humble, and here's what happened...

____

____

God Hunt

Today, I saw God show up when...

____

____

DATE: ______________________

Makeover Challenge

I tried my Makeover Challenge to become more humble, and here's what happened...

____

____

God Hunt

Today, I saw God show up when...

____

____

DATE: ______________________

Makeover Challenge

I tried my Makeover Challenge to become more humble, and here's what happened...

____

____

God Hunt

Today, I saw God show up when...

____

____

DATE: ____________________

Makeover Challenge

I tried my Makeover Challenge to become more humble, and here's what happened...

____

____

God Hunt

Today, I saw God show up when...

____

____

DATE: ____________________

Makeover Challenge

I tried my Makeover Challenge to become more humble, and here's what happened...

____

____

God Hunt

Today, I saw God show up when...

____

____

CHAT ABOUT IT

From your Makeover Journal, share a time you saw God last week, and discuss whether or not the God Hunt helped you avoid focusing on yourself. How did you do on the Makeover Challenge you selected (doing something nice in secret, receiving a compliment with a simple "thank you," complimenting someone irritating, or being receptive to advice)?

This week we're talking about the game show *Don't Forget the Lyrics!* On this show, the beginning of a song is played, and then the contestant has to fill in the missing lyrics. Many of the competitors can't sing worth a darn, but that doesn't matter—they just have to know the words!

If you could choose any type of contest, what kind of competition would you be most likely to win?

WHAT'S PLAYING ON YOUR IPOD?

The type of contest you said you'd be able to win signals an area where you feel *confident*. When you're engaged in that activity, you're probably telling yourself things like, "I can do this. I'm good at it. I enjoy this." We call this *positive self-talk*.

But sometimes we don't feel so confident. The messages in our minds may sound like this: "I'm a failure. I'll never get it. Why even try?" This is *negative self-talk*—and when we talk to ourselves like that, we feel insecure. And the more insecure we feel, the more we start faking it to cover up whatever we're insecure about!

You can choose your self-talk just like you choose what songs to put on your iPod. When you listen to a song over and over, you'll eventually memorize it word-for-word. You'll find the song running through your mind without even realizing it. Similarly, whatever self-talk you replay becomes a habit. If your self-talk is negative, you'll always feel insecure. But if you speak and think positively about yourself, you'll believe what you say to yourself—which will make you feel more confident!

CHECK YOURSELF

Today, we're going to compete in a Head-to-Soul version of *Don't Forget the Lyrics!* We're calling it *Don't Replay the Lyrics!* Instead of challenging ourselves to remember song lyrics, we're going to figure out what kind of self-talk is playing on the iPods of our minds.

Try *Don't Replay the Lyrics!* now. If you already took it online, refer to your printed results.

In Don't Replay the Lyrics! *instead of filling in song lyrics, you are completing thoughts with your typical self-talk. For each of the following situations, choose the self-talk that you tend to hear "replaying" on the iPod of your mind.*

1. When I'm feeling insecure, I tell myself…

- ☐ God created me and loves me just the way I am. [I accept myself.]
- ☐ My friends like me this way, so I must be okay. [I gauge my worth by what others seem to feel about me.]
- ☐ I'm insecure, PLUS I'm lonely, PLUS I'm having a bad hair day. [When I feel insecure about one thing, I find additional reasons to feel even more insecure.]

2. When I blow it, I tell myself…

- ☐ Everyone makes mistakes. Just admit it and try again. [I forgive myself.]
- ☐ I hope no one noticed! If anyone saw this, I'm dead. [I get embarrassed.]
- ☐ I am such a loser. [I call myself names.]

3. When I have a big problem, I tell myself…

- ☐ I know I'll figure something out. [I'm usually positive.]
- ☐ This isn't fair. I wish this weren't happening to me. Why me? [I usually question.]
- ☐ There's no way I can get through this. I give up! [I usually despair.]

4. When it comes to my choices, I tell myself…

- ☐ I've got to do what is right, even if my friends don't agree. [I'm independent.]
- ☐ I'll do whatever my friends are doing. [I'm a copier.]
- ☐ I do my best to try to make people happy, whatever it takes. [I'm a people-pleaser.]

5. **When I do something that's hurtful to a friend, I tell myself…**
   - ☐ I hate to hurt people. I'll have to apologize. [I own it.]
   - ☐ They're going to be so mad at me! They'll never forgive me. [I transfer my guilt to others and assume the worst.]
   - ☐ I'm going to beat myself up over this. I'll never forgive myself. [I punish myself.]

6. **When someone criticizes me, I tell myself…**
   - ☐ I'm still okay as a person, but maybe I need to listen and make some corrections. [I can find help in criticism.]
   - ☐ I feel like that person doesn't like me any more. [I take criticism as a personal attack.]
   - ☐ I am devastated! I know I disappoint people, and this just confirms it. [Criticism freaks me out.]

7. **When I'm new in a group, I tell myself…**
   - ☐ I wonder if there's anyone here I could get to know? [I reach out.]
   - ☐ Are they looking at me? Do they think I don't belong here? [I get self-conscious.]
   - ☐ This is so awkward! I wish I never came. I'll sit in the back and leave early. [I retreat.]

8. **When a friend genuinely compliments me, I tell myself…**
   - ☐ Wow! She's right! How awesome is that? [I receive compliments.]
   - ☐ That makes me uncomfortable. I don't like being the center of attention. [I feel awkward.]
   - ☐ She's so wrong. How could she possibly think that of me? [I reject compliments.]

9. **When I think about who I am, I tell myself…**
   - ☐ I have some great strengths, and some weaknesses that I'm working on. [I'm realistic.]
   - ☐ If I failed that day, I'm a failure. If I had a good day, I'm alright. [I flip-flop, based on circumstances.]
   - ☐ I am whatever my worst critics say I am. [I play their messages over and over in my mind.]

10. When I think about what I look like, I tell myself...

- ☐ There may be things I don't love about my looks, but I don't obsess about it. [My looks usually help me feel confident.]
- ☐ Mom says, "You have a great personality, dear!"—but that's not what guys go for. [My looks don't do my confidence any favors.]
- ☐ I wish I could hide my hair/complexion/weight/looks. [I obsess about my imperfections.]

11. When I think about being loved, I tell myself...

- ☐ God created me in his image and loved me enough to die for me. [I am lovable.]
- ☐ I feel best about myself when I have a boyfriend or best friend around. [I need affirmation.]
- ☐ I have a hard time believing I'm really loved for who I am. [I feel unworthy.]

12. When it comes to my past, I tell myself...

- ☐ What's past is past, and with God's help I can overcome my pain. [I let things go.]
- ☐ If my friends knew about my past, they'd think differently of me. [I cover things up.]
- ☐ My past feels like a trap. I'm stuck in patterns I can't change or get out of. [I feel imprisoned by my past and unable to change.]

13. When it comes to being different from my peers, I tell myself...

- ☐ I know my values and identity. What others believe or do doesn't really faze me. [I can stand alone.]
- ☐ It's important to have tolerance and avoid hurting people's feelings. [I don't speak out.]
- ☐ It would be better if I went along with what they're doing. [I conform.]

14. When I'm thinking about how I fit in with people, I tell myself...

- ☐ I feel relatively confident today, and on most days. [I am normal.]
- ☐ I scan the room and compare myself with everyone to see how I measure up. [I habitually rate myself.]
- ☐ Pretty much everyone I know is more confident/pretty/popular/successful/happy than I am. [I feel inferior.]

Confidence Scale

Shade in the number of boxes checked to see a visual scale of how confident, vulnerable, or insecure you are.

CONFIDENT: Total of all first boxes

1	2	3	4	5	6	7	8	9	10	11	12	13	14

UNCERTAIN: Total of all second boxes

1	2	3	4	5	6	7	8	9	10	11	12	13	14

INSECURE: Total of all third boxes

1	2	3	4	5	6	7	8	9	10	11	12	13	14

Key:

- **If you are Confident** in your self-talk, you reassure yourself, accept yourself, and embrace your strengths. You are real.
- **If you are Uncertain** in your self-talk, you question yourself, look to others for your cues, and rely on what other people say about you to establish how you feel about yourself.
- **If you are Insecure** in your self-talk, you are negative, you bash yourself, and call yourself names that make you feel defeated. You fake it in order to cover up your insecurities.

Some of you share from your Confidence Scale whether you are confident, uncertain, or insecure.

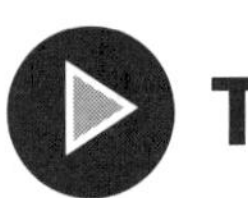

TRY IT OUT

Fill in some examples of the kind of self-talk you're replaying on the iPod of your mind.

I LOOK ______________

I WISH ______________

I FEEL ______________

I'M NOT ______________

I AM ______________

____

MENU

TALK IT OVER

CONFIDENCE-BUILDING LYRICS

Words that play over and over again in your mind are a primary influence on your confidence, so it's important that what you say about yourself agrees with what God says about you. So, what's so bad about self-talk that doesn't agree with what God thinks of you? Look at this progression of steps that can happen:

> **Step 1:** You start with self-talk that conflicts with what God says about you. Your talk is full of negativity—statements like "I'm shameful," "I'm unworthy," "I'm worthless," "I'm ugly," "I'm a failure," "I'm unforgivable."

Step 2: You begin to believe your self-talk.

Step 3: Since you believe your self-talk, you feel you have to hide the parts of you that you feel ashamed of, so you wear masks, cover up, hide, pretend.

Step 4: You become more and more FAKE!

So, if you want to "become real in a fake world," you need to start over at Step 1 and change your self-talk to what God tells you to say to yourself. Read this verse from Philippians aloud together:

> *Whatever is true, whatever is noble, whatever is right, whatever is pure, whatever is lovely, whatever is admirable—if anything is excellent or praiseworthy—think about such things.* (Philippians 4:8)

If this list of qualities to focus on in yourself could become a list of songs, you could think of this as your "confidence playlist"! So let's look at each of these confidence-building tracks on our playlist, and see how to get real with ourselves and stop being fake.

▶ **WHATEVER IS TRUE:** When you tell yourself whatever is true (or real), that means telling yourself what God says about you, instead of what someone else says.

> *Then you will know the truth, and the truth will set you free. (John 8:32)*

What kinds of negative things do you say about yourself that are easily proven wrong (such as, "I can't do anything right")? Do you need to let go of something bothersome someone else said about you that just isn't true?

▶ **WHATEVER IS NOBLE:** No matter how unworthy you may feel, God's love for you can't be shaken.

> *"Though the mountains be shaken and the hills be removed, yet my unfailing love for you will not be shaken nor my covenant of peace be removed," says the Lord, who has compassion on you.* (Isaiah 54:10)

In what situations do you tell yourself you are worthless or unlovable? What can you find in yourself that is noble (noble means "worthy of honor or respect")?

▶ **WHATEVER IS RIGHT:** God promises to take care of you if you're mistreated by someone.

> *Though my father and mother forsake me, the Lord will receive me. (Psalm 27:10)*

What kind of wrong has been done to you that has you telling yourself that your life isn't fair? What right thing can you start telling yourself about this situation instead?

▶ **WHATEVER IS PURE:** Nothing you have done is beyond the reach of God's cleansing power.

> *Long ago, even before he made the world, God chose us to be his very own through what Christ would do for us; he decided then to make us holy in his eyes, without a single fault—we who stand before him covered with his love.* (Ephesians 1:4 TLB)

What kinds of things make people feel impure, dirty, or unacceptable? Have you ever had a time when you told yourself you have done something that cannot be forgiven? Were you right?

▶ **WHATEVER IS LOVELY:** God wants to replace your injured, broken, or ugly places with beauty.

> *Those who look to him are radiant; their faces are never covered with shame.* (Psalm 34:5)

When you think about your appearance, is there anything about yourself that you would not necessarily call "lovely"? What does Psalm 34:5 say we can do to overcome our feelings of shame and look "radiant," or beautiful? Have you ever seen someone who has this quality of inner radiance that shines from inside? Describe what you think gives the person that radiance.

▶ **WHATEVER IS ADMIRABLE:** God gives you the power to do things you might not feel capable of accomplishing on your own.

> *I have strength for all things in Christ who empowers me—I am ready for anything and equal to anything through him who infuses inner strength into me, that is, I am self-sufficient in Christ's sufficiency!* (Philippians 4:13 AMP)

In what kinds of situations do you feel like you can't lead the way, that you're afraid to speak from your heart, or that you need to shrink to the background? What can you tell yourself at times like that?

▶ **IF ANYTHING IS EXCELLENT:** God's love and care for you proves your level of excellence in his eyes.

> *Look at the ravens—they don't plant or harvest or have barns to store away their food, and yet they get along all right—for God feeds them. And you are far more valuable to him than any birds!* (Luke 12:24 TLB)

Do you feel like you're unworthy or worthless? Do you tell yourself that you're just average? If you could put yourself in God's place, what do you think he would tell you right now about your worth?

- **OR PRAISEWORTHY:** God made us acceptable, which results in praise to him.

> *To the praise of his glorious grace, by which he has made us accepted in the Beloved.* (Ephesians 1:6 KJV)

When someone compliments you, do you feel you don't really deserve kindness, praise, or affirmation? When someone praises you, whom are they really praising? Why?

CHECK IN WITH YOUR MAKEOVER TEAM

Share with your team what you learned about how confident or insecure you are from *Don't Replay the Lyrics!* In this week's Makeover Journal, help one another come up with new self-talk statements and write them on your iPods. Arrange to connect with one another this week, and say your statements out loud together. It might feel silly, but just try it, and tell each other, "We are becoming real!"

MAKEOVER JOURNAL WEEK 3

CHOOSE A MAKEOVER CHALLENGE

Mark the three types of positive self-talk you need the most. These are the areas where you tend to "fake it" in order to cover up something. Write some new positive self-talk statements that you can play back on the iPod of your mind, using the three types of positive self-talk you selected. Say these things out loud to yourself at least once a day, and soon, instead of faking it, you'll be REAL! In your Makeover Journal, record what self-talk plays on the iPod of your mind when certain things happen in your day.

- ☐ **Whatever is true:** I need to let go of a lie someone said about me and believe God.
- ☐ **Whatever is noble:** I need to affirm that God loves me even when I feel embarrassed.
- ☐ **Whatever is right:** I need to remember God will take care of the wrong done to me.
- ☐ **Whatever is pure:** I need to declare that God says I am forgivable.
- ☐ **Whatever is lovely:** I need to see the beauty God has given me for my 'ashes.'
- ☐ **Whatever is admirable:** I need to claim God's power when I feel incapable.
- ☐ **If anything is excellent:** I need to state that I'm valuable when I feel average.
- ☐ **Or praiseworthy:** I need to thank God that I'm acceptable when I feel undeserving.

MY NEW POSITIVE SELF-TALK STATEMENTS

I LOOK ______________

I WISH ______________

I FEEL ______________

I'M NOT ______________

MENU

I AM ______________

____

DATE: ______________

Today, if people heard the iPod of my mind, this is the self-talk they would have heard...

____

____

Here is a message from God I can remember to support my positive self-talk and replace any negative self-talk...

____

____

DATE: ______________________

Today, if people heard the iPod of my mind, this is the self-talk they would have heard...

____

____

Here is a message from God I can remember to support my positive self-talk and replace any negative self-talk...

____

____

DATE: ______________________

Today, if people heard the iPod of my mind, this is the self-talk they would have heard...

____

____

Here is a message from God I can remember to support my positive self-talk and replace any negative self-talk...

____

____

DATE: ____________________

Today, if people heard the iPod of my mind, this is the self-talk they would have heard...

____

____

Here is a message from God I can remember to support my positive self-talk and replace any negative self-talk...

____

____

DATE: ____________________

Today, if people heard the iPod of my mind, this is the self-talk they would have heard...

____

____

Here is a message from God I can remember to support my positive self-talk and replace any negative self-talk...

____

____

DATE: ____________________

Today, if people heard the iPod of my mind, this is the self-talk they would have heard...

____

____

Here is a message from God I can remember to support my positive self-talk and replace any negative self-talk...

____

____

DATE: ____________________

Today, if people heard the iPod of my mind, this is the self-talk they would have heard...

____

____

Here is a message from God I can remember to support my positive self-talk and replace any negative self-talk...

____

____

EPISODE 4

Fear or Faith factor

CHAT ABOUT IT...

Last week we talked about replacing your negative self-talk with positive self-talk to build confidence and get more real with yourself.

Do you recall any moments this week when you caught yourself replaying an old negative message in your mind? Describe what happened.

This week we'll be considering *Fear Factor*, where contestants have to find the courage to face terrifying challenges to compete for a prize.

For you, which of the following actual stunts from the show *Fear Factor* would take the most courage?

1) Being locked in a box and covered with tarantulas
2) Eating wormy hotdogs and maggoty fried chicken
3) Leaping from one suspended beam to another, 20 stories in the air
4) Crouching for hours in a small, dark, enclosed septic tank with deafening sirens and occasional electric shocks

WHAT'S YOUR FEAR FACTOR?

People tend to react in a number of different ways to situations they find threatening—and that's true not just on reality shows but also in real life. Take a look at these three types of behavior that we're calling "fear factors":

- **STRESSING OUT** is when you can't stop worrying about something that might happen. *Stressing out takes over your thoughts and drains your energy.*
- **FREAKING OUT** is a common way of reacting when you feel threatened by people or situations you can't control. *Freaking out fills you with dread and causes you to shut down or lash out.*
- **HIDING OUT** is when you cover up your fear, which can take the form of denial, retreat, or lying. *Hiding out leads to deeper deception as you try to escape a consequence or cover your insecurity.*

CHECK YOURSELF

In our Head-to-Soul Makeover version of the show, which we call *Fear or Faith Factor,* we're going to put you through a test to reveal the way you typically react in situations you find threatening.

Do the *Fear Finder Test* now, or use your online results from www.headtosoulmakeover.com

FEAR FINDER TEST

What is your fear factor? When you're in a tense situation, you experience some sort of fear reaction. Imagine yourself in the following situations, and look at a typical fear reaction you could have. Rate how much you experience each type of reaction:

0 = I never or hardly ever react this way.

1 = I react like this every once in a while.

2 = I sometimes react this way.

3 = This is how I tend to react most often.

LIST A: STRESSING OUT

Situation		Fear Reaction
Being a visitor	☐	I get very self-conscious. I'm afraid I'll look awkward and sit alone.
Going to an unsafe area	☐	I obsess about all the possible threats and danger.
Being too busy	☐	My worry escalates, especially about what I'm *not* getting done.
Trying to make friends	☐	I think too poorly of myself, so I imagine I'll be ignored or rejected.
Taking a risk	☐	I'm afraid to try because I might fail.
A painful past	☐	I have a hard time letting go of my past. It affects me to this day.
I have abandonment issues	☐	I don't trust. I expect to be left or hurt by anyone I trust.
I failed	☐	I am filled with regret; I keep punishing myself.

LIST B: FREAKING OUT

Situation	Fear Reaction
I feel insecure	☐ I make myself even more anxious by comparing myself to others.
Speaking in public	☐ I'm terrified I'll forget my words and make a fool of myself.
I push myself	☐ I can never relax—there's always something I'm not getting done.
I deal with pain	☐ I get pain-focused—it's hard to think about anything else.
I'm overwhelmed	☐ I don't sleep well. I feel anxious that I'm feeling anxious!
My life is changing	☐ I don't do well with change—it can push me over the edge.
I feel out of control	☐ The more uncontrollables in my life, the more headaches, stomach problems, and other physical ailments I develop.
I have phobias	☐ Fear of heights, fear of spiders, claustrophobia, etc.

LIST C: HIDING OUT

Situation		Fear Reaction
I said something I regret	☐	When discussing it later, I rephrase what I said to make it sound not so bad.
I don't meet expectations	☐	I hide my shortcomings in order to avoid criticism.
I failed	☐	I have a hard time apologizing and admitting I was wrong.
I succeeded	☐	I downplay it, afraid I'll have to live up to expectations I can't meet.
I embarrass easily	☐	I cover up my embarrassment so they won't whisper about me.
I made a mistake	☐	I fix the mistake and hide the evidence so no one will know.
The real me isn't worthy	☐	I hide who I really am so they'll accept me or like me.
I'm a Christian	☐	I avoid talking about my beliefs with non-Christians.

Scoring

Your highest score on the Fear Finder Test is the fear reaction you tend to use under stress.

List A Points:	**Stressing Out:** You react to fear by **obsessing** about what *might* happen.
List B Points:	**Freaking Out:** You react to fear with **apprehension** that can cripple you.
List C Points:	**Hiding Out:** You react to fear by **covering up** your true self.

According to the *Fear Finder Test*, what is your most common reaction to threatening situations—stressing out, freaking out, or hiding out? Share a time when you reacted to stress using one of these "factors."

TALK IT OVER

FAITH FACTORS

Just about every person in the Bible exhibited some type of fear factor when facing stressful situations. In response, each of them had to learn a "faith factor"—a spiritual tool (such as prayer, trust, or truth) they could use to combat their fears. Let's look at three of those people, and the faith factors they used to overcome their fears.

TRY IT OUT

According to the results of your *Fear Finder Test*, divide into three teams based on where you scored the highest: If you scored highest on List A, fear can make you one of the *Stressed-Out Sisters*; a high score on List B places you among the *Freaked-Out Friends*; and List C means you're part of the *Hide-Out Homegirls*. In your teams, discuss your Bible story, then come back together and teach the rest of the group what you learned about your Bible character's fear factor and faith factor.

TEAM 1: THE STRESSED-OUT SISTERS

Stress Situation: Someone Needs Help. One of the greatest stories of courage in the Bible is the dramatic story of Esther. The three central characters of the story are Esther, an orphan who hides her Jewish heritage and then wins a beauty contest that makes her queen; Haman, an officer of the court who plots to kill all Jews because of one man who would not bow to him; and Mordecai, the courageous Jew who refuses to bow, and whose stirring words challenge Esther to face her fears and take action to save the Jews from disaster.

After Queen Esther learns about Haman's plot to destroy the Jews, her Uncle Mordecai asks her to go before her husband, the king, and plead with him to save her people (See Esther 4:8). Facing this situation where someone desperately needs her help, Esther is also forced to face her own fears.

Think of a situation in your life where you know someone needs help. Maybe it's someone who's being bullied at school, a friend in a difficult home situation, or someone struggling due to poverty or racial tensions. What kind of courage would it take for you to take action and do something to help that person or that group of people?

Fear Factor: Stressing out. Esther's first reaction was to stress out. Her mind started playing out the bad things that might happen if she went in to see the king. (There was a law that said that any person who approached the king without first being called by him could be put to death.) And the fact that the king hadn't asked to see Esther in a month made her even more stressed (See Esther 4:11).

What type of situation is most likely to trigger your fear reaction of stressing out?

Faith Factor: Prayer. When Esther realized she would die anyway if Haman's plot succeeded, she asked all the Jews to fast and pray with her for three days (See Esther 4:16). During this time, the Lord gave her the plan that eventually saved the Jews.

Here is what happens when we use the Faith Factor of prayer:

> *FAITH FACTOR VERSE: Do not be anxious about anything, but in everything, by prayer and petition, with thanksgiving, present your requests to God. And the peace of God, which transcends all understanding, will guard your hearts and your minds in Christ Jesus.* (Philippians 4:6-7)

What kinds of things that haven't happened yet do you worry about? When you're stressing out, how can this Faith Factor of prayer help you deal with it?

When your team gathers again with the rest of the group, explain to the group what stressing out is, what caused Esther to stress, and what faith factor she used to combat her worry. Share one example from your team's own experiences about how your faith factor verse can help you in a specific situation you have encountered.

TEAM 2: THE FREAKED-OUT FRIENDS

Stress Situation: Facing someone scary. David was the kid brother of a group of not-so-kind big brothers. When he went to visit his brothers on the battlefield, not only did he end up facing Goliath alone, but he also had to face the criticism and ridicule of his own older brother (See 1 Samuel 17:28). Threatening enemies are scary, and so are overcritical relatives!

Is there anyone in your life who is threatening, bullying, or overcritical? What kind of fear reaction do you have around them?

Fear Factor: Freaking out. Actually, David himself never freaked out. It was his brothers and the entire Israelite army who were getting more and more anxious every day because of this terrifying giant they couldn't control, couldn't face, and couldn't get away from (See 1 Samuel 17:11, 24).

What type of situation is most likely to trigger your fear reaction of freaking out?

Faith Factor: Trust in God's Power. David declared the reason for his courage: "The Lord who rescued me from the paw of the lion and the paw of the bear will rescue me from the hand of this Philistine" (1 Samuel 17:37). David remembered God's power in the past, and knew God would help him in the present. Then he used his skill and killed Goliath with his slingshot. This could have been the time David wrote the psalm where we find this verse:

> *FAITH FACTOR VERSE: In God, whose word I praise—in God I trust and am not afraid. What can mere mortals do to me?* (Psalm 56:3-4)

When you're feeling so afraid that you're freaking out, how can the Faith Factor of trust in God's power help you have courage? What has God already given you that you can use when you face bullies, critics, or difficult situations?

When your team gathers again with the rest of the group, explain what freaking out is, what caused the Israelite army to freak out, and what faith factor David used to combat fear. Share one example from your team about how your faith factor verse can help you in a specific situation you have encountered.

TEAM 3: THE HIDE-OUT HOMEGIRLS

Stress Situation: Resisting peer pressure. Daniel was alone in his daily habit of praying. His jealous co-workers tried to use his faith against him by pressuring him to shift his worship from God to the king. They figured he'd refuse, so they made a law that he'd be forced to break in order to keep him from getting the promotion that they wanted for themselves (See Daniel 6:4-9).

Do you face any pressure from people to compromise in your behavior or deny what you believe? How do you deal with that?

Fear Factor: Hiding out. Daniel could have been tempted to hide his habit of praying by closing the windows or praying at night. Hiding your beliefs is a way of lying or deceiving others.

What type of situation is most likely to trigger your fear reaction of hiding out?

Faith Factor: Truth. Daniel faced his fear by living truly. He kept praying three times a day, in full view of the court (See Daniel 6:10). His open and honest practice of his faith got him a night with the lions, but God kept him safe and he was set free.

> FAITH FACTOR VERSE: *Then you will know the truth, and the truth will set you free. (John 8:32)*

Describe a situation in your life where you need to live truly or speak the truth. This could be a situation where you cover up to protect yourself, where you're faking it to hide your true self, or where you're keeping a secret about something you or someone else is doing that is immoral, unethical, or dangerous.

When your team gathers again with the rest of the group, talk about what hiding out is, what could have caused Daniel to hide, and what faith factor he lived by instead. Share one example from your team about how your faith factor verse can help you in a specific situation you have encountered.

CHECK IN WITH YOUR MAKEOVER TEAM

Share with your team what your Fear Factor is and what kinds of situations cause you to have that kind of fear reaction. Go to your Makeover Journal for this week and choose your Makeover Challenge; share with your team which one you chose and why. Pray for one another about the situations in which you need more courage, and to remember to turn your own fear into prayers. Set a time to check in with one another this week and read one another at least one of the worry prayers you've written in your Makeover Journal.

MAKEOVER JOURNAL, WEEK 4

CHOOSE A MAKEOVER CHALLENGE

Choose a challenge based on which Fear Factor you want to overcome. Try the Bonus Challenge, too! Be sure to refer to the Faith Factor Verses to help you with your Makeover Challenge this week.

If my Fear Factor is...	...I will apply a Faith Factor and...
Stressing out	☐ **Befriend someone.** I will stop worrying about what people think of me and be friendly to a stranger I encounter during my day, or someone whom I've been avoiding because she or he seems to be so needy or scary.
Freaking out	☐ **Try an experience.** I will stop letting fear keep me from taking risks, and say "Yes!" to a new experience that I would normally avoid (such as helping at church, trying Persian food, or holding a snake!)
Hiding out	☐ **Keep a truth journal.** I will develop the courage to speak truthfully by keeping a list of the times I tell the truth, even when it might be tempting to mislead, cover up, or lie.

MAKEOVER BONUS CHALLENGE: TURN FEARS INTO PRAYERS

Turn your worried thoughts upward and tell them to God in prayer. Keep a list in your Makeover Journal this week of the fears you turned into prayers—you could even write out your prayers and go back and read them if you start worrying again. Share your prayers online in this week's Makeover Blog, and get ideas by reading other prayers at www.headtosoulmakeover.com.

DATE: ______________________

Makeover Challenge

Today, I overcame a Fear Factor when I showed courage by...

____

____

Turn Fears into Prayers

Dear Lord, today I'm worried about...

____

____

DATE: ______________________

Makeover Challenge

Today, I overcame a Fear Factor when I showed courage by...

____

____

Turn Fears into Prayers

Dear Lord, today I'm worried about...

____

____

DATE: ______________________

Makeover Challenge

Today, I overcame a Fear Factor when I showed courage by...

____

____

Turn Fears into Prayers

Dear Lord, today I'm worried about...

____

____

DATE: ______________________

Makeover Challenge

Today, I overcame a Fear Factor when I showed courage by...

____

____

Turn Fears into Prayers

Dear Lord, today I'm worried about...

____

____

DATE: ______________________

Makeover Challenge

Today, I overcame a Fear Factor when I showed courage by...

____

____

Turn Fears into Prayers

Dear Lord, today I'm worried about...

____

____

DATE: ________________________

Makeover Challenge

Today, I overcame a Fear Factor when I showed courage by...

____

____

Turn Fears into Prayers

Dear Lord, today I'm worried about...

____

____

DATE: ________________________

Makeover Challenge

Today, I overcame a Fear Factor when I showed courage by...

____

____

Turn Fears into Prayers

Dear Lord, today I'm worried about...

____

____

EPISODE 5

CHAT ABOUT IT

Last week's Courage Challenge may have pushed you to try something new. Share how you befriended someone, tried a new experience, or told the truth when tempted to lie. Did you try the Bonus Challenge of turning fears into prayers? Look back at the prayers you recorded in your Makeover Journal and share how that worked for you.

Dig down for some major self-control, because you're about to compete on *The Biggest Loser.* This weight-loss show is all about resisting temptation and exercising self-discipline. At the final weigh-in, the person who has done the best job of transforming his or her body with a new healthy lifestyle is the winner.

Let's talk about different temptations—which of these would be hardest for you to resist? Why?

(1) A refrigerator full of your favorite foods when you're trying to diet.

(2) Facebook messages from four friends when you're supposed to be studying.

(3) A group of girls gossiping about a person you have a story about.

(4) Buying something you love even though you have other things like it.

WHAT DO YOU NEED TO LOSE?

Our version of *The Biggest Loser* goes beyond losing weight. On our Head-to-Soul version of the show, becoming a *Total Loser* means exercising self-control and successfully losing your greatest area of temptation:

- **LOSE THE MOUTH:** If you are easily provoked or unkind, you need self-control over your speech.
- **LOSE THE ATTITUDE:** If you follow your impulses or give in to self-centeredness, you need to exercise self-control over your attitude.
- **LOSE THE APPETITE:** If a habit is controlling you and making you compromise, you need to exercise self-control over the appetites that drive you.

CHECK YOURSELF

Let's just make sure of one thing before we go on. This week, when we call ourselves "total losers," that's a good thing! We don't want to revert back to the negative self-talk and start calling ourselves "losers" as a way of putting ourselves down. This is the one time you can call yourself a "total loser" and it means something admirable!

When we go on *Total Loser*, the first thing we have to do is "weigh in" to see what we have to lose.

Do the *Total Loser Weigh-In* now, or weigh-in online at www.headtosoulmakeover.com.

WEIGH-IN

What is the biggest thing you need to lose? Exercising self-control is the way to become a Total Loser, *whether that means losing hurtful words, selfish attitudes, or bad habits. Weigh yourself on three scales, giving each statement 0 to 4 pounds, in order to see where you need to become a* Total Loser.

0 pounds = I never have this issue

1 pounds = I hardly ever have this issue

2 pounds = I sometimes deal with this issue

3 pounds = I frequently struggle with this issue

4 pounds = I usually have a real problem with this issue

SCALE 1: LOSE THE MOUTH
(UNCONTROLLED WORDS AND EMOTIONS)

____ I tend to say hurtful things to people without even realizing it.

____ If I'm having a bad day, I take it out on my family or friends.

____ I enjoy a good gossip session with the girls.

____ I snap at people and get irritated easily.

____ I interrupt people and finish their sentences.

____ I get critical if I don't agree with what someone's doing.

____ I use swear words, or I use the name of God or Jesus as an expression.

____ I speak before I think, which gets me into trouble.

____ I tend to be judgmental, regularly jumping to conclusions or voicing a negative opinion.

____ I tend to overreact. My emotional levels go from one extreme to the other.

SCALE 2: LOSE THE ATTITUDE
(UNCONTROLLED IMPULSES AND SELF-CENTEREDNESS)

____ I get stressed because I take on too much.

____ I am a drama queen—I exaggerate how wonderful or terrible things are.

____ I might disobey my parents if I think their rules don't make sense.

____ I might break a rule at school if I think it doesn't make sense.

____ I hold a grudge—it's hard for me to let go of a hurt.

____ I tend to show off, especially if I accomplish something worth bragging about.

____ I tend to complain—I can find something wrong with just about anything.

____ I am a bit reckless—I act before I think, which gets me into trouble.

____ I procrastinate, putting off things I don't feel like doing.

____ I act religious, but I'm not sure I really buy into the whole God-thing.

SCALE 3: LOSE THE APPETITE (LACK OF WILLPOWER)

____ I usually do whatever the group is doing and have a hard time resisting temptation.

____ I consume too much caffeine, or diet pills, or energy drinks, or alcohol.

____ I have trouble disciplining myself to work or do something I don't feel like doing.

____ I am obsessed with exercise, or dieting, or my looks.

____ I engage in more relaxation than I need (television, Facebook, sleep).

____ I stay too long in relationships that drag me down.

____ I do not have a balanced diet, and I eat to comfort myself.

____ I don't have good work habits—I'm lazy, I get distracted, I go on Facebook instead of doing my homework.

____ I have a habit (shopping, gambling, chat rooms, partying, etc.) I can't control.

____ I "treat myself" too much (Starbucks, buying clothes, taking a break from work, etc.).

WEIGH-IN

Add your pounds on each scale to see where you need to be a Total Loser.

Scale 1: 'Lose the Mouth' Total Pounds: _______

Scale 2: 'Lose the Attitude' Total Pounds: _______

Scale 3: 'Lose the Appetite' Total Pounds: _______

When you "weighed in," in what area did you have the most "pounds" to lose? Can you think of anything that happened recently where you could have exercised more self-control?

TALK IT OVER

BEFORE AND AFTER PICTURES

The most captivating part of the reality show *The Biggest Loser* is when you get to see side-by-side comparisons of photos of contestants at the beginning of the show and at the end, 15 weeks later. The difference in the way a person looks after losing weight and getting healthier can be amazing.

Our *Total Loser* show invites us to an amazing change in our behavior. For example, a person who starts off with little or no self-control and "lets it all hang out" is not very attractive. She may say things like, "I always say what I think," or "What you see is what you get," or "I can't help the way I am." To this person, being "real" means being a real mess, because she just doesn't have the willpower to be any other way. But our show is all about losing the attitude and behaviors that weigh us down. Let's check out some 'Before' and 'After' pictures of the different types of "losers," as found in a few of Paul's letters in the New Testament.

TRY IT OUT

As we go through our lesson, we'll come back and fill in these 'Before' and 'After' pictures.

LOSE THE MOUTH

"BEFORE" PICTURE

A person who needs to "lose the mouth" does not have a very pretty "Before" picture in this passage. Consider this description from Colossians where Paul suggests some traits worth losing:

> *But now is the time to get rid of anger, rage, malicious behavior, slander, and dirty language.* (Colossians 3:8, NLT)

When are you most likely to have trouble controlling your speech? (Think about how you speak when you're stressed, angry, hurt, tired, embarrassed, or frustrated.) On the "Before" picture, write in the type of speech you have trouble controlling (gossip, anger, criticism, crude language, etc.)

"AFTER" PICTURE

Now let's take a look at the "After" picture. As this passage is read aloud, circle the action words that show how our speech can be transformed.

> *Let the words of Christ, in all their richness, live in your hearts and make you wise. Use his words to teach and counsel each other. Sing psalms and hymns and spiritual songs to God with thankful hearts. And whatever you do or say, let it be as a representative of the Lord Jesus.* (Colossians 3:16-17, NLT)

This passage suggests four things you can do to get control of your speech. What are they, and how can each one actually help you control your speech?

On the "After" picture, write in one of these actions you'll use to control your speech.

LOSE THE ATTITUDE

"BEFORE" PICTURE

When you don't have self-control of your impulses or your self-centeredness, it can look pretty scary. Read this passage:

> *For people will love only themselves and their money. They will be boastful and proud, scoffing at God, disobedient to their parents, and ungrateful...They will be unloving and unforgiving; they will slander others and have no self-control... They will betray their friends, be reckless, be puffed up with pride, and love pleasure rather than God. They will act religious, but they will reject the power that could make them godly.* (2 Timothy 3:2-5, NLT)

Pick out the traits of a self-centered person from this passage—how many can you find?

Select one of the traits in this "Before" description that you are most likely to show when you're acting self-centered, and describe how it looks on you. Write it in the heart on your "Before" picture.

"AFTER" PICTURE

After you lose the attitude, you'll be "wearing" something different. Here's what you'll look like:

> *You must clothe yourselves with tenderhearted mercy, kindness, humility, gentleness, and patience. You must make allowance for each other's faults, and forgive anyone who offends you. Remember, the Lord forgave you, so you must forgive others. Above all, clothe yourselves with love, which binds all together in perfect harmony.* (Colossians 3:12-14, NLT)

What are the items in your new spiritual wardrobe that you'll be putting on for your "After" picture? How can these "clothes" help you lose your self-centered attitude? Write one or more of these characteristics in the heart on your "After" picture.

LOSE THE APPETITE

"BEFORE" PICTURE

Here's something that's tough to lose—your appetite for things that are bad for you...in other words, a bad habit. If a habit has power over you, here's what needs to happen:

> *So put to death the sinful, earthly things lurking within you. Have nothing to do with sexual immorality, impurity, lust, and evil desires. Don't be greedy, for a greedy person is an idolater. Because of these sins, the anger of God is coming.* (Colossians 3:5-6, NLT)

The first line of this passage uses some strong words to describe what you must do to lose your habit. What are they? (Say them with feeling!) Why is it necessary to be so harsh with bad habits? Think of an appetite you have that's bad for you, and write it on your "Before" picture.

"AFTER" PICTURE

Again, being a "loser" means taking off old clothes and putting on a new wardrobe, but this time it's more like an extreme makeover. Look at the "After" picture:

> *You have stripped off your old evil nature and all its wicked deeds. Put on your new nature, and be renewed as you learn to know your Creator and become more like him.* (Colossians 3:9-10)

Tell the story of when you became clothed in your new nature. (That's another way of saying, "Tell how you became a Christian.") How has the presence of Christ in your life helped you "lose the appetite"? Write that on your "After" picture.

CHECK IN WITH YOUR MAKEOVER TEAM

Go deeper with your Makeover Team by sharing a specific area from the *Total Loser Weigh-In* where you need more self-control. Go to your Makeover Journal for this week and choose your Makeover Challenge; share with your team which one you chose and why. Connect with one another this week and say, "You're a Total Loser!" Then, seriously cheer for the other members of your team as you all make progress in exercising self-control.

Special Note: *If you have not had the most extreme makeover of all, which is to invite Jesus Christ into your life so he can transform you into a new person, now is your chance! Your Makeover Team and your leader will pray with you.*

MAKEOVER JOURNAL WEEK 5

CHOOSE A MAKEOVER CHALLENGE

Be a Total Loser *by choosing the Makeover Challenge in the area where you need to lose the most and exercise the most self-control. Remember, the goal isn't to try to be someone you're not. Instead, the goal is to let go of any destructive behaviors that keep you from living out your true nature as a child of God. Keep track of your progress in your Makeover Journal or your online blog.*

If you scored highest in...	...try this Makeover Challenge to develop more self-control.
Lose the Mouth	☐ **Pray before you speak.** Try stopping and praying this verse before you say something you'll regret: "Set a guard over my mouth, Lord, keep watch over the door of my lips" (Psalm 141:3, TNIV).
Lose the Attitude	☐ **Resist a temptation.** Do the right thing even when you don't feel like it. This may mean obeying your parents, doing your homework, or not following the crowd.
Lose the Appetite	☐ **Start a new habit.** Replace your old habit with a new one, such as eating healthy, reading a chapter in Proverbs every day, or memorizing a verse to help you when you're tempted, like Romans 6:19.

DATE: ____________________

Today, I was a "Total Loser" when I exercised self-control by...

____

____

DATE: ____________________

Today, I was a "Total Loser" when I exercised self-control by...

____

____

DATE: ____________________

Today, I was a "Total Loser" when I exercised self-control by...

____

____

DATE: ____________________

Today, I was a "Total Loser" when I exercised self-control by...

____

____

DATE: ____________________

Today, I was a "Total Loser" when I exercised self-control by...

____

____

DATE: ____________________

Today, I was a "Total Loser" when I exercised self-control by...

____

____

DATE: ____________________

Today, I was a "Total Loser" when I exercised self-control by...

____

____

CHAT ABOUT IT

See who was a *Total Loser* this past week by sharing stories about exercising self-control over your mouths, your attitudes, or your habits. Look over your Makeover Journal and share a time where you tried praying before speaking, resisting a temptation, or starting a new habit.

Today's reality show may be the most unnerving one of all. We're calling it *LifeSwap*, and it's based on *WifeSwap*—a show where two wives trade families for two weeks. The experience of living with people who are very different from you can be a supreme test of patience.

Which of the following real families from the show *WifeSwap* would be the most irritating for you to live with?

(A) The Galvans, where a controlling mom picks which clothes everyone wears every day, sets a timer for how long the kids brush their teeth, inspects every room daily to make sure everything's perfectly clean, and listens in on everyone else's phone calls.

(B) The Haigwoods, who raise their own food on their farm and eat it all raw (even the meat), don't believe in school (or home schooling), never buy anything new (they barter or buy used), and never eat in restaurants.

(C) The Roys, whose home is out-of-control chaos: Mountains of laundry, rooms where the floor can't be seen because of the mess, burping contests, public rudeness, frequent pranks, constant television, and absolutely no chores for anyone.

WHEN ARE YOU MOST IMPATIENT?

This week as a contestant on our show, *LifeSwap*, you'll be put into the living situation you find most irritating given your particular personality. It's a good thing we emphasized self-control last week, because you'll need to have control of your speech and your attitudes in order to exhibit patience toward others. *LifeSwap* gives you opportunities to exercise patience with...

- **IRRITATING PEOPLE:** Let's face it. Even if you are the most self-controlled person in the world, some people are just irritating. It can take patience to understand and love certain people.
- **PET PEEVES:** We all have certain things that are guaranteed to annoy us. How you deal with your everyday annoyances tells a lot about how patient you are.
- **WAITING:** On the show *WifeSwap*, the women who switch homes must each live for a week with the other family's lifestyle before making any changes. It's not until the second half of the visit that the wives can make the rules everyone has to live by. If you find it hard to wait to get what you want, to see changes, or to gain control of a situation, then you need more patience.

CHECK YOURSELF

Okay. Brace yourself. *LifeSwap* is about to begin. Let's look at some irritating situations to find out where you most need to develop more patience.

Take the *LifeSwap Test* now or take the online version at www.headtosoulmakeover.com.

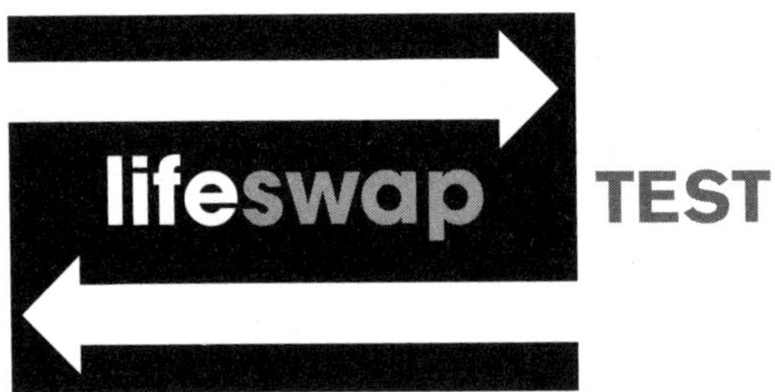

TEST

If you had to do a LifeSwap *and were forced to be with irritating people, endure your pet peeves, or wait for something you wanted, you would need a lot of patience. Select your biggest frustrations, then rate how you do at being patient with them.*

IRRITATING PEOPLE

Check the type of person you'd find most irritating to have to live with for two weeks—or write in an idea of your own.

- ☐ A negative person who always complains
- ☐ A liar who is untrustworthy
- ☐ A person who always has a better story or a worse day than yours
- ☐ An incessant talker who never asks about you
- ☐ A bossy person who always has to be in charge
- ☐ Other____

Oh no! That irritating person is in the family you are assigned for your LifeSwap! Circle the place on each scale that reflects how strongly you would lean toward one behavior or the other around that person.

1 2 3 4 5 6 7 8 9 10

I am irritable — I am kind

1 2 3 4 5 6 7 8 9 10

I judge that person — I try to understand why he or she is like that

1 2 3 4 5 6 7 8 9 10

I react in anger — I ignore small insults

1 2 3 4 5 6 7 8 9 10

I try to control that person — I try to love that person

1 2 3 4 5 6 7 8 9 10

I feel miserable when I think about that person — I have let go and moved on

PET PEEVES

Check the type of pet peeve that most annoys you—or write in your own idea.

- ☐ Being interrupted by a parent making you do a chore "right now"
- ☐ Losing something and having to look everywhere for it
- ☐ Cleaning up someone else's mess
- ☐ People who talk loudly on cell phones
- ☐ People who have annoying habits
- ☐ Other____

The members of your LifeSwap family repeatedly do your most annoying pet peeve. Circle the place on each scale that reflects how strongly you would lean toward one reaction or the other.

1 2 3 4 5 6 7 8 9 10

I get frustrated quickly — I take a deep breath and chill

1 2 3 4 5 6 7 8 9 10

I get rather self-centered — I put others before myself

1 2 3 4 5 6 7 8 9 10

I complain, either aloud or to myself — I find something positive to say

1 2 3 4 5 6 7 8 9 10

I feel sorry for myself — I shrug my shoulders and forget it

1 2 3 4 5 6 7 8 9 10

I get angry when my expectations aren't met — I let go of my expectations

WAITING

In WifeSwap, *contestants must wait one week before implementing their way of doing things. In life, there are many kinds of waiting. Check the kind of waiting that is hardest for you— or write in your own idea.*

- ☐ Waiting for the day of a fun event you've been anticipating
- ☐ Being delayed or asked to stop moving forward on your plan
- ☐ Waiting for the right time to confront someone or say something you need to say
- ☐ Waiting to make a decision until you have evaluated it enough
- ☐ Waiting for your friend to forgive you and reconcile with you
- ☐ Other____

Imagine the time you spend waiting in the situation you have circled. Circle the place on each scale that reflects how strongly you would lean toward one way of handling waiting or the other.

1 2 3 4 5 6 7 8 9 10

I get antsy and nervous — I release my need to control my schedule

1 2 3 4 5 6 7 8 9 10

I get depressed and feel far from God — I use the delay to pray

1 2 3 4 5 6 7 8 9 10

I act before I think — I think before I act

1 2 3 4 5 6 7 8 9 10

I do what feels good — I wait to make sure I'm doing what is right

1 2 3 4 5 6 7 8 9 10

I get confused and anxious — I wait until I have peace

LIFESWAP SCORE

Now, add up each section. Your lowest score is the area where you are the most impatient.

Irritating People ______ Pet Peeves _______ Waiting _______

In what area of patience do you need to do the most work? What additional ideas did you write in?

TRY IT OUT

A TEST OF PATIENCE

Divide into teams and take two minutes to see which team can build the tallest house out of cards. After you're done, consider these questions:

People work on problems in different ways. What did you observe about how others on your team tried to build a house of cards differently from you? Did you find yourself reacting with patience or impatience at these differences?

In what ways does a house of cards remind you of pet peeves?

What role does waiting play in building a house of cards?

TALK IT OVER

DO AN INTERNAL LIFESWAP

Instead of doing an **external** *LifeSwap* where we exchange families and endure situations that cause us impatience, we're going to try an internal *LifeSwap*, where we swap our impatience for God's patience. Like the second half of *WifeSwap*, in which the women get to set up new rules for the families they've been living with, *you* get to make the rules in your *LifeSwap*. Here are some new rules you can try to increase your patience with people, pet peeves and waiting.

LIFESWAP YOUR IRRITATION FOR GOD'S LOVE

If you're struggling to deal with people who irritate you, instead of lashing out at them, or gritting your teeth and hiding your feelings, try out these three new rules to help you have patience.

RULE 1: GIVE THEM UNDERSTANDING.

Try to understand people before getting irritated with them—you may discover an explanation for their behavior. **There's a connection between patience and understanding.**

> *Those who are patient have great understanding.*
> (Proverbs 14:29)

In what kinds of situations can **understanding** help you have patience with irritating people?

RULE 2: GIVE THEM A BREAK.

Even if you can't find any explanation for someone's behavior, overlook those faults by loving that person. **There's a connection between patience and love.**

> *Be patient with each other, making allowance for each other's faults because of your love.*
> (Ephesians 4:2 NLT)

In what kinds of situations can **love** help you have patience with irritating people?

RULE 3: GIVE THEM WHAT YOU'VE RECEIVED.

When you stop and think about it, God has had to exhibit far more patience with you over your lifetime than you have to show to the person you're irritated with at the moment. **There's a connection between patience and mercy.**

> *But God had mercy on me so that Christ Jesus could use me as a prime example of his great patience with even the worst sinners.* (1 Timothy 1:16)

In what kinds of situations can **mercy** help you have patience with irritating people?

LIFESWAP YOUR ANNOYANCE FOR GOD'S SELFLESSNESS

Before we talk about the new rules for pet peeves, first let's find out what it is that annoys you.

What are your pet peeves? See how many things you can think of that trigger your impatience.

So, when your pet peeves strike again, try these new rules (they're all from one verse in the "love chapter" of the Bible) to de-peeve those annoying 'pets'!

RULE 1: LET GO OF YOUR WAY.

Pet peeves are really nothing more than little moments of selfishness. Learn to let go of your agenda, your preferences, your expectations.

> *[Love is] never haughty or selfish or rude. Love does not demand its own way.* (1 Corinthians 13:5a, TLB)

Thinking back to your list of pet peeves, what is the link between selfishness and your pet peeves? How can you exercise patience instead?

RULE 2: LET GO OF YOUR PITY PARTY.

Impatient people tend to let pet peeves get to them quickly, especially when they're tired, frustrated, sick, or feeling sorry for themselves.

> *[Love] is not irritable or touchy.*
> (1 Corinthians 13:5b, TLB)

Are there certain situations in which you become irritable more quickly than at other times? How can you be patient in those times?

RULE 3: LET GO OF YOUR GRUDGE.

Sometimes pet peeves are best handled by not paying attention to them. Learn to let something slide, overlook an insult, or stop noticing every little thing someone does wrong.

> *[Love] does not hold grudges and will hardly even notice when others do it wrong.*
> (1 Corinthians 13:5c, TLB)

Can you think of a way to apply this verse to times when your pet peeves make you impatient?

LIFESWAP YOUR UNREST FOR GOD'S PEACE

Do you find it hard to wait? Here are your new rules to help you find peace while you're waiting.

RULE 1: DON'T JUST DO SOMETHING—STAND THERE!

If you get presumptuous and assume God is late, you might decide to do something just to be doing *something!* You might make a snap decision, go with what feels good, or jump the gun and act even when the direction isn't clear.

> *God makes everything happen at the right time.*
> (Ecclesiastes 3:11, CEV)

In what situations have you felt like God was late? How does this verse—and this rule—help you not jump the gun?

RULE 2: DON'T FRET—PRAY.

Delays and roadblocks are there for a reason. Instead of stewing and fretting about what you should do, use the delay to pray. When you see the phrase "wait on the Lord," it usually means to pray while you wait!

> *Be still before the Lord and wait patiently for him; do not fret...* (Psalm 37:7)

How can prayer help you when you hit roadblocks along your way?

RULE 3: DON'T DECIDE IF YOU DON'T HAVE PEACE.

Don't steamroller over the roadblock or panic about your confusion. Invite God to stand there with you, and don't make a move until he releases you to do so by giving you peace.

> *For God is not a God of disorder, but of peace.*
> (1 Corinthians 14:33)

What kinds of delays have you experienced? How can this rule help you handle these situations?

CHECK IN WITH YOUR MAKEOVER TEAM

Go back to your *LifeSwap* survey and share what makes you most impatient. Then choose the Makeover Challenge you'll work on in your journal this week. Share with your team which challenge you chose and why. Pray for one another about being patient. Set up a time and a way to connect during the week to encourage one another as you try out your internal *LifeSwap*. Try out the daily reminders at www.headtosoulmakeover.com to help you remember your *LifeSwap* challenge. This one could be the hardest of all!

MAKEOVER JOURNAL WEEK 6

CHOOSE A MAKEOVER CHALLENGE

Do an internal LifeSwap *this week, choosing the Makeover Challenge that addresses the area where you most need to develop more patience. Refer back to the verses mentioned in the* LifeSwap *rules to help you. Keep track of your progress in your Makeover Journal.*

If you have the hardest time with…	…try this Makeover Challenge to develop more patience.
Irritating People	☐ **Get to know the people who irritate you.** If you are habitually impatient with certain people, find out their interests, their pet peeves, the things that bring them joy or sadness. *LifeSwap* your irritation for God's love.
Pet Peeves	☐ **Don't sweat the little things…**and most of the things that bug us are little things. Purposefully let go of something that would normally annoy you. *LifeSwap* your annoyance for God's selflessness.
Waiting	☐ **Build in a pause.** Use the time to check in with God and see if he wants you to stay silent, to wait on your decision, or to pray until you have peace. *LifeSwap* your unrest for God's peace.

DATE: ______________________

Today, I did an internal *LifeSwap* and showed patience by...

____

____

DATE: ______________________

Today, I did an internal *LifeSwap* and showed patience by...

____

____

DATE: ______________________

Today, I did an internal *LifeSwap* and showed patience by...

____

____

DATE: ______________________

Today, I did an internal *LifeSwap* and showed patience by...

____

____

DATE: ______________________

Today, I did an internal *LifeSwap* and showed patience by...

____

____

DATE: ______________________

Today, I did an internal *LifeSwap* and showed patience by...

____

____

DATE: ______________________

Today, I did an internal *LifeSwap* and showed patience by...

____

____

EPISODE 7

CHAT ABOUT IT

Did you write anything in your Makeover Journal last week about getting to know someone who would normally irritate you, purposefully ignoring a pet peeve, or pausing before a decision? Share a situation where you exercised more patience than usual.

Here's the show you've been waiting for...you are being featured on *My Super Sweet 16!* This show follows real-life teenagers as they prepare to celebrate their sixteenth birthday with a party where no expense is spared! Here's what you might experience on the show:

- A Fantasy-Land party, where you make a grand entrance dressed in a showgirl costume and riding on an elephant, with a complete carnival, and a gift of a Range Rover.
- A Diamonds Are Forever party, where you're carried in on the shoulders of two hulking men, and given a 7-carat diamond ring and a $100,000 Mercedes sedan.
- The Fairy Tale party in a castle tent, where you arrive in a Cinderella carriage, have knights as your bodyguards, see a fireworks show in your honor, and receive the gift of a new BMW.

What kind of theme would you want for your ideal Super Sweet 16 party? If you could have the party anywhere in the world, where would you hold it? Who would be your guest performer? What kind of food would you serve? What would you wear?

MY SUPERFICIAL SWEET 16

My Super Sweet 16 is an entertaining—and sometimes sickening—look at the tantrums and meltdowns that some very rich girls have in the process of receiving a party that's lavish beyond imagination. These girls are bent on creating for themselves what could be called the most fake world of all—a world where they get everything they want, and they go to extremes to appear popular. It's all supposed to be super—but usually it just ends up feeling *superficial*. Here are three types of superficiality, as shown in these exact quotes from girls on the show:

- **I WANT IT ALL:** This is the girl who grasps for every *thing*—from jewels to clothes to cars—and declares, "I'm used to getting everything I want, and if I don't...look out."
- **IT'S ALL ABOUT ME:** This girl thrives when the world revolves around her: "I love being the center of attention, when everything's focused on me."
- **HOW DO I RATE?** This girl obsesses about comparing herself to others: "I have to stand out among everyone else, and I have to be the hottest thing at my party."

Each of these girls got what she wanted—the gifts, the attention, the status. So, why weren't they satisfied? Because each of them was trying to find happiness in something superficial.

CHECK YOURSELF

Well, you're about to be featured on our Head-to-Soul version of the show. We're calling it *My Superficial Sweet 16*. Right now, you'll find out how content you are as you rate how superficial or super-satisfied you'd feel in various situations.

Take the *My Superficial Sweet 16 Tally* now or online at www.headtosoulmakeover.com.

TALLY

Do you look for happiness in superficial things like possessions, attention, or status? Find out just how superficial or super-satisfied you are by selecting how you'd be most likely to respond in each situation.

1. Your friend just got a new iPhone, and you don't have one. How do you respond when she's showing it off?
   a. I wish I could convince my parents to get me an iPhone.
   b. I change the subject and tell about something new I got recently.
   c. I think about some way in which I am luckier than her, and that makes me feel better.
   d. I'm happy for her and I ask to see how the phone works.

2. You are working on a group project. How do you act?
   a. I'll do whatever it takes to get a good grade, and I'll make sure I get the grade I deserve even if other group members flake out.
   b. I want to be in charge of the group, because it seems like my ideas are better than other people's.
   c. I find myself evaluating who is doing how much work to make sure everything's fair.
   d. I contribute my best work for the good of the group, and I try to be affirming and encouraging of other group members along the way.

3. You need a new pair of jeans. What is your shopping tactic?
   a. I look for a name brand that will impress my friends.
   b. I take my friends with me and buy the jeans they say look best on me.
   c. I look at what the hot girls are wearing and try to buy that.
   d. I buy the jeans that I feel best in and that I can afford.

4. You are having friends over. You know their houses are bigger than yours. How do you feel about your house?
   a. I am embarrassed because I don't think my house is good enough.
   b. I just wish my parents would give me a private area where my friends and I could hang out and have fun.
   c. I think about a friend's house and wish my house was like hers.
   d. Even though my house isn't perfect, I enjoy sharing it with my friends.

5. Your friend is talking about the dinner her family had together. Your family hasn't eaten together since Christmas. How does her talk make you feel?
   a. I can't relate. My family isn't like that—and I wish it was.
   b. I'm depressed. I say my family never has dinner together, and I hope people notice how sad I am.
   c. I think she's so lucky. Everything about her family sounds so perfect, and I imagine they always get along.
   d. I'm interested in her experience, and I ask questions about how the dinner went.

6. A group of your friends decide to go to a concert, but you're not allowed to go because it's on a school night. How do you react?
   a. I have a meltdown because this was a once-in-a-lifetime opportunity, and I mope around for the rest of the night.
   b. I complain to my friends about my strict parents and hope to get a little sympathy.
   c. I feel jealous and wish I had cool parents like everyone else. It's unfair that they got to go and I didn't.
   d. Although I was disappointed I couldn't go, I enjoy looking at my friends' pictures and hearing about their fun evening.

7. You are at the Homecoming game. Which of these activities are you most likely to do?
   a. I look at the football players and daydream about going out with one of them.
   b. I envy the homecoming queen because she's the center of attention and seems so popular.
   c. I gossip about the cheerleaders and check out who's sitting with who.
   d. I enjoy the game and have fun with my friends.

8. You are having lunch at school. Which of these things happens most often?
   a. I eye my friend's cute outfit and think about what I need to go out and buy.
   b. I pull out my mirror to check how I look.
   c. I envy the couples around me.
   d. I eat my lunch and enjoy my friends.

9. A popular girl walks by. What goes through your mind?
   a. I check out what she's wearing and wish I could shop where she does.
   b. I think about how many friends she has and how happy she must be, and I wish I could trade places with her.
   c. I find something to criticize about her.
   d. I admire her, and something about her makes me just say a quick prayer for her.

10. It's Friday night, and you have nothing to do. What do you tell yourself about that?
    a. I can't sit still. I have to come up with something to do or I'll go crazy.
    b. How humiliating. How could I have a Friday night by myself? Everyone has forgotten about me, and they don't care that I'm all alone!

c. What's wrong with me? I'm sure they're all out together and they left me out on purpose.

d. I love having an evening to myself to kick back and relax!

SO...ARE YOU SUPERFICIAL OR SUPER-SATISFIED?

Add up all your A's, B's, C's and D's to find the answer!

OOPS! I'M SUPERFICIAL!

Total A's______ **I Want It All!** I am most likely to be discontent with what I have and think I'll be happy if I get more things.

Total B's______ **It's All About Me!** I am most likely to think I'd be happier if I were more popular.

Total C's______ **How Do I Rate?** I am most likely to compare myself with other people and think I'd be happier if I were like them or better than them.

GUESS WHAT? I'M SUPER-SATISFIED!

Total D's______ I am most likely to feel happy a lot of the time be cause I'm content with who I am and what I have.

In what areas do you tend to be the most discontent?

TRY IT OUT

THE CONTENTMENT EXPERIMENT

As a way of illustrating how contentment works, your leader is going to pass out a variety of items to the group. After you receive an item imagine that you *are* the item you've been given. Think about these questions:

What is it about being this item that you are dissatisfied with?

Look around and choose someone else's item that you would rather be. Why would you choose to be that item?

Shift your thinking now, and list reasons why you are thankful you are this item.

What can you learn about contentment from this exercise?

TALK IT OVER

THREE WAYS TO GET SUPER-SATISFIED

There are three kinds of behavior that lead to discontentment: Coveting things, comparing yourself to others, and being jealous of attention. If you want to become real in a fake world, you will work on replacing these types of discontentment with super-satisfaction. Then you will be a genuine person—and more likeable too!

1. CHOOSE CONTENTMENT OVER COVETING

In our Contentment Experiment we started by complaining about things we were dissatisfied with. It can become a habit to look at our circumstances and always wish things were different.

There's a famous story that describes exactly what can happen when we covet (long for or crave) what we don't have. It's one of Aesop's Fables—maybe you even read it as a child. In the story of "The Dog and the Shadow," a dog walks across a bridge, carrying a piece of meat in his mouth. Looking down he sees his own reflection in the water. He thinks, "That dog has a mighty fine-looking piece of meat, and I want it!" So the dog snaps at the shadow in the water—but when he opens his mouth, the piece of meat he had drops into the water and is lost. The moral of the story is: *If you covet all, you may lose all.*

What kinds of things do you find yourself wishing for? When have you become so preoccupied with what you don't have that you stop enjoying what you do have?

The Bible describes what happens when you love things too much.

> *But godliness with contentment is great gain. For we brought nothing into the world, and we can take nothing out of it. But if we have food and clothing, we will be content with that. Those who want to get rich fall into temptation and a trap and into many foolish harmful desires that plunge people into ruin and destruction. For the love of money is a root of all kinds of evil.* (1 Timothy 6:6-10)

Imagine that you must choose between a million dollars and contentment. Which would you choose—and why?

What does this passage say is a "trap"? How do we avoid that trap?

2. STOP COMPARING AND START REJOICING

The next part of our Contentment Experiment was to compare your item with someone else's, and think about why you'd rather have the other item. Another word for that desire for what someone else has is *envy*, and *envy* starts with comparison. Whenever you find you're comparing yourself to someone else, watch out! You're headed for one of two problems. If you compare and say, "I didn't get what she got—that's not fair!" then you can easily get *jealous*. If you compare and say, "She doesn't have what I have—sure glad I'm not her," then you get *prideful*. How do you stop comparing? Try to follow this advice:

> *Rejoice with those who rejoice, and weep with those who weep.* (Romans 12:15, NASB)

Which part of this verse is harder for you—to be happy with others when they are happy, or to be sad with them when they are sad? How does rejoicing with those who rejoice cure jealousy? How can it cure pride?

3. IT'S NOT ALL ABOUT ME...IT'S ALL ABOUT YOU!

Joseph's brothers had a problem. Ever since their baby brother Joseph was born, he was their father's favorite. He got all the attention, he never did anything wrong, and he even got a special gift from Dad that no one else received—a coat of many colors. His brothers were so jealous, they got rid of Joseph by selling him into slavery. (See Genesis 37 for the rest of Joseph's exciting story.)

Have you ever envied someone who was the center of attention? Do you ever do things in order to become the center of attention, to be more popular, or to be loved?

If we were able to talk to Joseph's brothers, they might tell us they just wanted to feel special. They wanted their father's attention and approval, so they tried to get rid of anyone who was in their way. Instead of thinking about their youngest brother's well-being, or about how losing him would break their father's heart, they thought only of themselves. They said, "It's all about me." The cure for "It's all about me" is to turn it into "It's all about you." How? 1 Corinthians 13:4 tells us love is not jealous—it does not envy. In fact, love cancels out envy. Envy is all about *me*; love is all about *you*.

If Joseph's brothers had chosen to love Joseph instead of envying him, what might have happened between them and their father? Are there any situations in your family or at school in which loving others would work better for you than trying to make sure you are loved?

CHECK IN WITH YOUR MAKEOVER TEAM

Based on your assessment results, share with your team how superficial or super-satisfied you are. Go to your Makeover Journal for this week and choose your Makeover Challenge; share with your team which one you chose and why. Pray for one another about the areas where each of you needs to develop more contentment. Set up a time and a way to connect during the week to encourage one another and to read aloud at least one day's "16 Thank Yous." If you haven't been connecting during the week, figure out why, and make it happen this week!

MAKEOVER JOURNAL WEEK 7

CHOOSE A MAKEOVER CHALLENGE

Transform yourself into a super-satisfied person by choosing the Makeover Challenge that helps you be more content in the area in which you struggle. Keep track of your progress toward "becoming real in a fake world" in your Makeover Journal or online blog.

If you scored highest in...	...try this Makeover Challenge to become more content.
I Want It All	☐ **Have a "Stay at Home" Party.** Instead of going out, go through your house and find books you haven't read, games you haven't played, crafts you haven't done, or foods you've never tried. Try them out—and enjoy what you already have.
It's All About Me	☐ **Change Your Focus.** Seek to listen to others, let them have the spotlight, and quietly pray for them instead of jumping in and telling your story.
How Do I Rate?	☐ **Say "No" to Envy.** Do your best to "rejoice with those who rejoice" and genuinely show happiness for others when good things happen in their lives.

MAKEOVER BONUS CHALLENGE: 16 THANK YOUS

One great way to develop contentment is to work on being thankful for what you have already. Compete with yourself every day this week to try to say "thank you" for 16 different things per day. Give yourself one point for every time you thank God for something, and for every time you thank a person for anything throughout the day. (It might be your parent, a restaurant server, a teacher, your friend.) Keep score by making brief notes in your Makeover Journal, or by trying the online Thank-You Counter at www.headtosoulmakeover.com. If your whole group has at least five days of 16 Thank Yous this week, reward yourselves!

DATE: ______________________

Today, I became super-satisfied by being content when…

____

____

16 Thank Yous *(List the things for which you said thank you)*

1 __________ 2 __________ 3 __________ 4 __________
5 __________ 6 __________ 7 __________ 8 __________
9 __________ 10 __________ 11 __________ 12 __________
13 __________ 14 __________ 15 __________ 16 __________

DATE: ______________________

Today, I became super-satisfied by being content when…

____

____

16 Thank Yous *(List the things for which you said thank you)*

1 __________ 2 __________ 3 __________ 4 __________
5 __________ 6 __________ 7 __________ 8 __________
9 __________ 10 __________ 11 __________ 12 __________
13 __________ 14 __________ 15 __________ 16 __________

DATE: ____________________

Today, I became super-satisfied by being content when...

____

____

16 Thank Yous *(List the things for which you said thank you)*

1 __________ 2 __________ 3 __________ 4 __________
5 __________ 6 __________ 7 __________ 8 __________
9 __________ 10 __________ 11 __________ 12 __________
13 __________ 14 __________ 15 __________ 16 __________

DATE: ____________________

Today, I became super-satisfied by being content when...

____

____

16 Thank Yous *(List the things for which you said thank you)*

1 __________ 2 __________ 3 __________ 4 __________
5 __________ 6 __________ 7 __________ 8 __________
9 __________ 10 __________ 11 __________ 12 __________
13 __________ 14 __________ 15 __________ 16 __________

DATE: ____________________

Today, I became super-satisfied by being content when...

____

____

16 Thank Yous *(List the things for which you said thank you)*

1 __________ 2 __________ 3 __________ 4 __________
5 __________ 6 __________ 7 __________ 8 __________
9 __________ 10 __________ 11 __________ 12 __________
13 __________ 14 __________ 15 __________ 16 __________

DATE: ______________________

Today, I became super-satisfied by being content when…

____

____

16 Thank Yous *(List the things for which you said thank you)*

1 __________ 2 __________ 3 __________ 4 __________
5 __________ 6 __________ 7 __________ 8 __________
9 __________ 10 __________ 11 __________ 12 __________
13 __________ 14 __________ 15 __________ 16 __________

DATE: ______________________

Today, I became super-satisfied by being content when…

____

____

16 Thank Yous *(List the things for which you said thank you)*

1 __________ 2 __________ 3 __________ 4 __________
5 __________ 6 __________ 7 __________ 8 __________
9 __________ 10 __________ 11 __________ 12 __________
13 __________ 14 __________ 15 __________ 16 __________

EPISODE 8

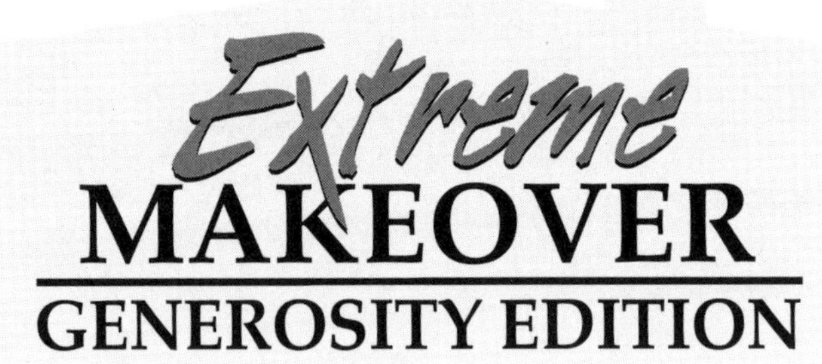

CHAT ABOUT IT

Let's start off by seeing how everyone did on the 16 Thank Yous Bonus Challenge. Share something about your experience of trying to be more thankful—how did it affect you? Did you find yourself feeling more content? Compare the number of thank yous that each of you said—and celebrate!

Now, look over the Makeover Challenge section of your journal and share how you practiced being more content this past week. Did you have a "stay at home" party and enjoy things you already have? Did you focus on others and resist telling your own story? Did you rejoice with those who were rejoicing?

This week you get to be part of the team on *Extreme Makeover: Home Edition.* This show finds a family that's going through a difficult time, and builds them a new house that will help give them a fresh start.

Which of the following members of the *Extreme Makeover* team would you most enjoy being and why?

- **The Team Leader (Ty):** He inspires the team and volunteers to meet big goals, and shows his own artistic flair by working the entire week by himself on a secret room for one family member.

- **The Carpenter (Paige):** In her pink hardhat and pink toolbelt, she has the carpentry skills to build beautiful kitchen cabinets and specialty furniture for children's rooms.
- **The Designer (Paul):** He has an amazing imagination, and his job is to design extravagantly themed rooms around each family member's hobbies.
- **The Shopper (Tracy):** Her role on the team is to go shopping! She acquires all the furniture and decor, and the useable items that fill the cupboards, closets, drawers, and walls.

LET'S DO IT!

After the *Extreme Makeover* team decides to take on a new project, they huddle, stack hands, and call out, "Let's do it!!!" And, wow, do they do it! It takes different types of generosity to get the job done:

- **Generosity with Talents:** We see all kinds of gifted people on the show, donating what they do best—decorating, hammering, planting, painting, organizing, even doing a musical performance.
- **Generosity with Time:** Hundreds of volunteers show up to help build a house in seven days. The people on the show are generous with their time, often working throughout the night to finish the job on time.
- **Generosity with Things:** Whenever you see the family given a special surprise gift—such as a new car, money to pay off a mortgage, or prepaid college education for the children—you know that behind it are generous people who are good at giving away their money and their things.

CHECK YOURSELF

On our *Extreme Makeover: Generosity Edition* show, you get to see which kind of generosity you do best. Are you most generous with your things, your talents, or your time?

Take the *Extreme Makeover: Generosity Edition Survey.*

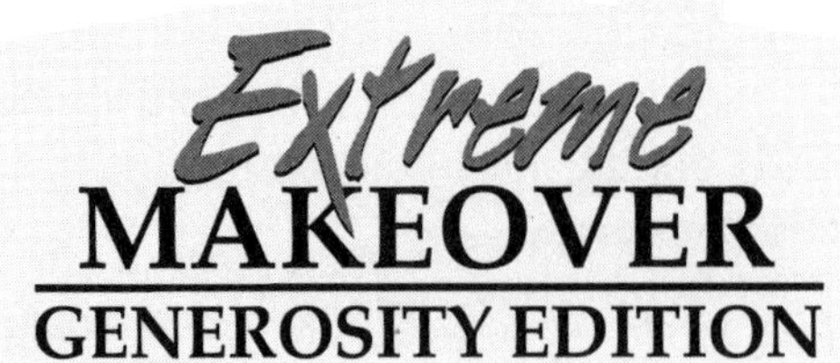

SURVEY

Do you use your things, your talents, and your time to help others—or only for your own good? If you are more "all about yourself" than about giving to others, then your generosity might need an Extreme Makeover. Circle the letter corresponding with your most honest answer to each question.

1. How do you respond to interruptions (phone calls, mom asking you to do something, sibling wanting something)?

   V I try to set aside what I'm doing and meet the person's need.

   T I usually feel impatient, because they are interfering with my agenda.

   D If the interruption is important, I set aside what I'm doing.

2. If a friend wants to borrow your favorite sweater, how do you feel?

   S As a rule I don't lend out my clothes or my stuff.

   G What's mine is yours! Enjoy using it!

   P I let her borrow it, but I feel nervous about it. I don't want it to be ruined or lost.

3. The new girl wants to join your group for lunch. How do you feel?

   C Awkward! What is she thinking? Our group is just too well-established, and she'll feel out of place.

   M I don't mind if she sits with us, but I wouldn't go out of my way to strike up a conversation with her. I usually let my more outgoing friends do that.

   H I'd welcome her, help her get to know everyone, and ask her about herself to try to help her feel comfortable.

4. When someone desperately asks for help with something you don't enjoy doing (cleaning up after an event, doing yardwork, taking care of kids, helping a friend study, etc.), what's your answer?

   D I'm not sure. Depends on what else I have to do.

   V I can always find time to help!

   T My schedule is too full.

5. When you hear about a tragedy (someone's house burned down, a starving orphan in Africa, flood victims), how do you respond?

   P I might see if my parents will send a check to help.

   G I try to figure out a way to raise money to help (go without something for a week, donate my allowance, organize a fundraising drive, etc.).

   S I feel sorry for them, but that's as far as it goes.

6. What do you do with your hobby?

   M My hobby gets me recognition (I perform; I enter contests; I make things to give to friends).

   C My hobby is mostly for my own enjoyment (I play my guitar in my room; I collect movie star memorabilia).

   H I use my hobby to help others (I make things to give away to needy people; I perform for groups to encourage them; I use my talent to help people).

7. What do you do at church?

   T I go to church now and then.

   D I go to church and youth services on a regular basis.

   V I do things for my personal spiritual growth, and I volunteer regularly (teach children, clean the building, lead worship, welcome visitors, work in the nursery, etc.).

8. The kid next to you in class keeps asking you for help. What do you feel?

    C Irritation, like, "Your stupidity is not my problem. Ask someone who cares!"

    H I try to help if it's appropriate. I like helping people.

    M Tolerance, like, "I'll help you this one time, but I wish you'd figure it out yourself."

9. How often do you volunteer in the community (visit a seniors' residence, feed homeless people, help in a kids' club, etc.)?

    T I have never really done that. I don't have time, or I don't know how to get involved.

    V At least once a month.

    D Once or twice a year.

10. What do you do with your money?

    P I use my money for entertainment and gas and clothes, and once in a while I give something in the church offering.

    S I only have enough money for my basic needs, so it all goes for that.

    G I give a percentage of my money to church or charity regularly, and the rest I save or spend.

11. Your mom asks if you'd be willing to babysit three kids on Saturday so your neighbor (a single mom) can get away for the day. What is your first thought?

    H How cool that there is something I can do to help!

    C Will she pay me?

    M What if I don't like her kids? Then it won't be any fun.

12. If you have two homemade cookies in your lunch, what do you do?

    G I automatically offer the second one to the person I'm sitting with.

    S I try to eat them in private so no one else will see them and ask for one.

    P If someone asks me for one, I'll give it away...reluctantly.

DOES YOUR GENEROSITY NEED AN EXTREME MAKEOVER?

Count each letter and see how generous you are. Scores of 3 or 4 are a strong trend.

Are you generous with your THINGS and money?

Total S's_______ **Stingy:** I hoard my things and don't like sharing.

Total P's_______ **Possessive:** I share when I have to, but you might have to pry my fingers loose.

Total G's_______ **Generous:** I don't view my things as my own, and I enjoy giving to bless others.

Are you generous with your TALENTS and skills?

Total C's_______ **Closed:** I'm closed to people and not willing to put myself out to meet the needs of others.

Total M's_______ **Me-centered:** If it's good for me, then I'll help.

Total H's_______ **Helpful:** I use my abilities for the good of others.

Are you generous with your TIME and agenda?

Total T's_______ **Time Hoarder:** My time is too precious to let other people infringe on my schedule.

Total D's_______ **Drifter:** My schedule fills up with whatever seems important or meets my needs that particular day.

Total V's_______ **Volunteer:** I purposefully give some of my time away on a regular basis.

Take a look at the areas where you scored 3 or 4 points. Do you see a strong generous trend (high G, H, or V), or do you have a stronger trend toward holding things for yourself (high S, C, or T)?

TRY IT OUT

GIVE A MAKEOVER...GENEROSITY-STYLE

Choose one group member to be the recipient of a generosity-style makeover, where all the other group members contribute in various ways to her makeover.

What kinds of generosity were exhibited?

How did it feel to show that kind of generosity?

Recipient: What was it like to receive that kind of generosity?

How did you feel about the fact that only one person received a makeover?

TALK IT OVER

THREE STEPS TO AN EXTREME GENEROSITY MAKEOVER

If you need to become more generous in some way, follow these three steps to an Extreme Generosity Makeover: Figure out the problem, follow the plan, and feel the pleasure.

STEP 1: FIGURE OUT THE PROBLEM

When the Extreme Makeover team arrives at a family's home, their first job is to figure out what's wrong with the house. In order to start our Generosity Makeover, we need to do the same thing. Match each of the following four Scripture passages with the greed-related problem that can block generosity.

Passage A: 1 Kings 21:2-4 Problem #____

Ahab said to Naboth, "Let me have your vineyard to use for a vegetable garden, since it is close to my palace...I will pay you what it is worth." But Naboth replied, "The Lord forbid that I should give you the inheritance of my ancestors." So Ahab went home, sullen and angry...He lay on his bed sulking and refused to eat.

Passage B: Luke 12:15 Problem #____

He [Jesus] said to them, "Watch out! Be on your guard against all kinds of greed; life does not consist in an abundance of his possessions."

Passage C: Ecclesiastes 5:10 Problem #____

Those who love money never have enough; those who love wealth are never satisfied with their income.

Passage D: Deuteronomy 8:10-18 Problem #____

When you have eaten and are satisfied, praise the Lord your God for the good land he has given you...Otherwise...your heart will become proud and...you may say to yourself, "My power and the strength of my hands have produced this wealth for me." But remember the Lord your God, for it is he who gives you the ability to produce wealth.

Problem 1: PRIDE

It's hard to be generous when you feel so proud of what you worked to gain and really want to hang onto it. But we don't really own our possessions, because even our ability to get what we have was given to us by God.

Problem 2: SELFISHNESS

If you're greedy, your life motto might be, "It's all about me." You shut out everyone else's needs and focus only on your own.

Problem 3: ANXIETY

A greedy person is characterized by anxiety. When you think you'll only be happy after you have the next thing or achieve the next success, you can never rest.

Problem 4: INSECURITY

If you think your self-worth is improved by what you own, what you wear, what you drive, or where you live, then greed is faking you out. Having more doesn't make you more secure.

Describe why one or more of these problems makes it hard for you to be generous. Try explaining the Scripture that goes with your problem in your own words.

STEP 2: FOLLOW THE PLAN

After the Extreme Makeover team figures out the problem, they make a plan for the new house—and then follow that plan as they build. We have a plan for generosity that we can follow, and we can read about it in the story of the poverty-stricken Macedonians in 2 Corinthians. Take a look at what Paul says about the sacrificial generosity the Macedonians expressed toward the persecuted church in Jerusalem. It's a three-part plan for being generous:

> *They are being tested by many troubles, and they are very poor. But they are also filled with abundant joy, which has overflowed in rich generosity. For I can testify that they gave not only what they could afford, but far more. And they did it of their own free will. They begged us again and again for the privilege of sharing in the gift for the believers in Jerusalem. They even did more than we had hoped, for their first action was to give themselves to the Lord and to us, just as God wanted them to do.* (2 Corinthians 8:2-5, NLT)

Part A: Don't be held back by what you lack. *They are being tested by many troubles, and they are very poor. But they are also filled with abundant joy, which has overflowed in rich generosity.* The Macedonians were tested by great troubles and were very poor. Yet, they gave much because of their great joy!

How have your troubles, or your feelings that you don't have enough to spare, kept you from being generous with your time, talents, or things?

Part B: Find the need that tugs your heart. *For I can testify that they gave not only what they could afford, but far more. And they did it of their own free will. They begged us again and again for the privilege of sharing in the gift for the believers in Jerusalem.* The Macedonians gave more than they could afford, even going so far as to beg and plead for the opportunity to share. They weren't just *faking* interest—they were passionately concerned about the plight of the persecuted church in Jerusalem.

What cause or ministry or need do you feel most passionate about? Why?

Part C: Money is fine...but give talents and time! *They even did more than we had hoped, for their first action was to give themselves to the Lord and to us, just as God wanted them to do.* The Macedonians surprised Paul by giving in a way he did not expect: They went beyond money and gave of themselves. Sometimes, generosity can be faked. Giving money or supporting a child in a developing country can look generous, but sometimes it can be just a way of taking care of guilt or looking good, which is prideful. Likewise you may go on a mission trip for the fun of being with friends, with no real desire to serve the local people. Being real in a fake world means being a *truly* generous, others-centered person.

Beyond your money, what do you have that you can give to the Lord and to others? Share some ways you have given your time or your talents to help others. Can you point to any times you have given with a wrong motivation?

STEP 3: FEEL THE PLEASURE

The "big reveal" at the end of a home makeover is exciting, because you see the joy on the faces of the family as they receive everyone's generosity. That's the cool thing about giving. You don't lose when you give; your joy multiplies!

> *If you give, you will receive. Your gift will return to you in full measure, pressed down, shaken together to make room for more, and running over.* (Luke 6:38, NLT)

Does this Scripture mean that whatever we give, we'll get the same thing back? How does the pleasure of giving compare with the pleasure of buying something for yourself? What does this verse mean to you, and how does it encourage you to be more generous?

CHECK IN WITH YOUR MAKEOVER TEAM

Share with your team how you rated on the *Extreme Makeover: Generosity Edition* assessment. Go to your Makeover Journal for this week and choose your Makeover Challenge, then share with your team which one you chose and why. Pray for one another about becoming more generous. Set up a time and a way to connect during the week to encourage one another and see how you're doing at letting go and being generous.

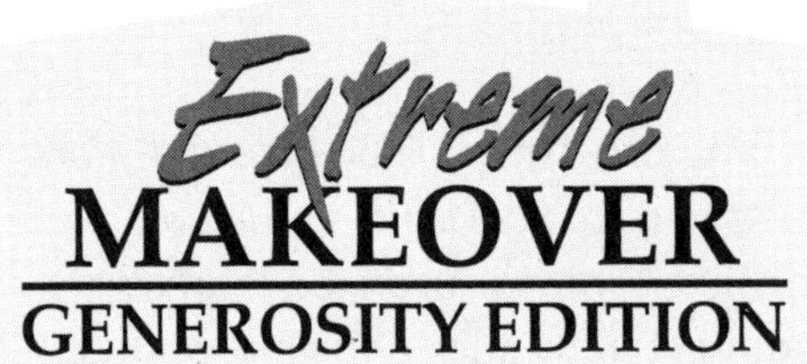

MAKEOVER JOURNAL WEEK 8

CHOOSE A MAKEOVER CHALLENGE

Try out your Generosity by choosing a Makeover Challenge that addresses the area in which you have the most trouble letting go. Write about how it feels to exercise that type of generosity in your Makeover Journal or online blog.

If it's hard being generous with your…	…try this Makeover Challenge to develop your generosity.
Things	☐ **Donate something.** I will give away things I don't use, OR I will volunteer at a facility that helps those who have less than I do. (Write about how it feels to help.)
Talents	☐ **Transform your hobby.** I will think of a way to use my hobby or talent to help others this week. (Write about how it feels to use your hobby in a new way.)
Time	☐ **Be interruptible.** I will treat interruptions as opportunities to be generous with my time by giving someone my focused attention as I listen to that person. (Write about how it feels to give up some of your time intentionally.)

DATE: ______________________

Today, I got a generosity makeover when…

____

____

DATE: ______________________

Today, I got a generosity makeover when…

____

____

DATE: ______________________

Today, I got a generosity makeover when…

____

____

DATE: ______________________

Today, I got a generosity makeover when…

____

____

DATE: ______________________

Today, I got a generosity makeover when…

____

____

DATE: ______________________

Today, I got a generosity makeover when…

____

____

DATE: ______________________

Today, I got a generosity makeover when…

____

____

EPISODE 9

THE *REALLY* AMAZING RACE

CHAT ABOUT IT

Refer to what you wrote in your Makeover Journal last week and share what it felt like to show generosity by donating something, transforming your hobby, or being interruptible.

This week you are competing on *The Amazing Race*. In this contest, teams race around the world, overcoming challenges and problems along the way.

Which of the following actual challenges performed by *Amazing Race* teams would you be most likely to quit, and what is it about it that would make it hard for you to finish?

1. Eating a whole bowl of caviar
2. Carrying a 55-pound side of raw beef a mile
3. Herding 1,000 ducks into a pen 50 yards away
4. Jumping into the hold of a boat and searching for a marked crab among 500 live crabs
5. Walking barefoot on a 220-foot path of jagged stones
6. Taking part in a local seafaring tradition that requires you to have "FF" (for "Fast Forward" challenge) permanently tattooed on your body

THREE REASONS QUITTERS QUIT

For our Head-to-Soul version of *The Amazing Race,* we're calling it *The* Really *Amazing Race*. This is a race that can't be won by a quitter. It definitely takes *perseverance* to overcome the three types of challenges teams encounter during every leg of the race:

- **DETOURS** are demanding tasks the team must do before moving on. Detours can cause *discouragement,* because you may try and fail, or you fear other people will do better than you.
- **A YIELD** is something one team can use to force another to stop for a while. Yields are like *criticism,* when people find things wrong with you and make it difficult for you to keep going.
- **ROADBLOCKS** are challenges that require extra exertion. Roadblocks often cause *frustration* from trying to learn something new, or getting so overwhelmed you lose hope.

CHECK YOURSELF

As you compete in *The* Really *Amazing Race,* it's important to discover which type of challenge is most likely to make you quit.

Take the *Quitter's Quiz* now, or online at www.headtosoulmakeover.com.

THE *REALLY* AMAZING RACE

THE QUITTER'S QUIZ

Quitters quit because of discouragement, criticism, or frustration. Think about things you have not finished—examples might include a class, a project, a volunteer job, a relationship, a conversation, a book, a chore, a dream. For each of the following typical reasons to quit, circle your rating:

I.Q. = I Quit
If this happens to a great enough degree, it would probably cause me to quit.

H.I.T. = Hang In There
Even if this happens frequently, I would probably hang in there.

THE DETOUR OF DISCOURAGEMENT

I.Q. **H.I.T.** **BLAME:** I made a stupid mistake, and I'm angry at myself.

I.Q. **H.I.T.** **COMPARISON:** The way I do it isn't as good as the way others do it.

I.Q. **H.I.T.** **MISUNDERSTOOD:** I feel misunderstood and unappreciated.

I.Q. **H.I.T.** **FAILURE:** I tried really hard, but I failed.

I.Q. **H.I.T.** **LAZINESS:** I just don't care anymore.

I.Q. **H.I.T.** **LONELINESS:** I feel all alone, with no one to help me when I need it.

I.Q. **H.I.T.** **LOSS OF INTEREST:** My initial enthusiasm has worn off.

I.Q. **H.I.T.** **OVERCOMMITTED:** I should have never taken this on.

I.Q. **H.I.T.** **POOR HEALTH:** I don't feel well, so I don't have much energy.

I.Q. **H.I.T.** **PROCRASTINATION:** I keep putting it off and avoiding it.

I.Q. **H.I.T.** **STRESSED OUT:** I feel overloaded—just too many things to do.

THE "YIELD" OF CRITICISM

I.Q. **H.I.T.** **CONFLICT:** I argue a lot with others.

I.Q. **H.I.T.** **DIFFICULT PERSON:** That person is hard to work with.

I.Q. **H.I.T.** **FEAR OF DISAPPOINTMENT:** I'm afraid I'll let someone down—or let myself down.

I.Q. **H.I.T.** **FEAR OF RESPONSIBILITY:** If I take this on and it doesn't work, others will blame me.

I.Q. **H.I.T.** **OTHERS' EXPECTATIONS:** I can't reach someone else's high standards.

I.Q. **H.I.T.** **PERSECUTION:** My beliefs are challenged or belittled.

I.Q. **H.I.T.** **PREJUDICE:** I am the object of discrimination or being pre-judged.

I.Q. **H.I.T.** **PUT DOWNS:** I get criticized no matter how hard I try.

I.Q. **H.I.T.** **REJECTION:** I got turned down by someone.

I.Q. **H.I.T.** **UNFAIR ACCUSATION:** I am being punished unjustly.

I.Q. **H.I.T.** **UNSUPPORTED:** A person who's important to me doesn't believe I can do it.

THE ROADBLOCK OF FRUSTRATION

I.Q. **H.I.T.** **CONFLICTING PRIORITIES:** Something else seems more important.

I.Q. **H.I.T.** **DIFFICULT LEARNING CURVE:** It's hard to learn this new skill/role/subject.

I.Q. **H.I.T.** **FEELS POINTLESS:** I don't have a clear goal or strong direction.

I.Q. **H.I.T.** **HOPELESSNESS:** The task is overwhelming.

I.Q. **H.I.T.** **LACK OF RESOURCES:** I don't have enough money/time/facilities/help.

I.Q. **H.I.T.** **LOSING:** I'm competitive, and I don't like not winning.

I.Q. **H.I.T.** **OUT OF CONTROL:** I'm not in charge, and they're not doing things the best way.

I.Q. **H.I.T.** **PAIN:** I have physical discomfort or pain.

I.Q. **H.I.T.** **PREVIOUS SUCCESS:** I did well before, but I may not be able to do it again.

I.Q. **H.I.T.** **TOO HARD:** I don't have the skills required for success.

I.Q. **H.I.T.** **UNCOOPERATIVENESS:** People aren't doing what they're supposed to.

THE QUITTER'S QUIZ SCORECARD

Add up your totals. The area with the highest "I.Q." is the type of problem that is most likely to make you quit.

	Total I.Q.'s	**Total H.I.T.'s**
Discouragement	______	______
Criticism	______	______
Frustration	______	______
Total ALL "Hang In Theres"		______

23-33 H.I.T.'s: *Your perseverance makes you "Most likely to finish the race."*

12-22 H.I.T.'s: *You might complete the race—but only if you don't encounter too many problems.*

1-11 H.I.T.'s: *You are voted "Most likely to quit, due to circumstances."*

Some of you share what type of quitter you are, and tell a story about a time you missed out on something because you quit. Why is the quality of perseverance so important in life?

TRY IT OUT

HOW TO PERSEVERE

Work together to complete the word search using the word list that relates to perseverance.

Place the remaining letters in the blanks to discover how to persevere.

G	H	R	E	N	N	I	W	C	E
E	T	O	U	P	O	D	E	O	M
N	T	E	P	M	N	P	T	M	O
E	R	E	V	E	S	R	E	P	C
O	A	H	R	M	U	I	L	E	R
E	I	S	T	A	C	Z	P	T	E
I	N	I	M	T	C	E	M	E	V
R	U	N	E	U	E	T	O	H	O
T	S	I	S	R	E	P	C	A	N
Y	O	F	U	E	D	F	A	L	L

COMPETE
COMPLETE
END
FINISH
HOPE
MATURE
OVERCOME
PERSEVERE
PERSIST
PRIZE
RUN
SUCCEED
TRAIN
WINNER

___ ___ ___   ___ ___   ___ ___ ___   ___ ___ ___ ___   ___ ___ ___ ___

___ ___ ___ ___ ___ ___ ___   ___ ___ ___ ___.

Why is this statement a key to persevering? Have you ever had a time in your life when you did this? Describe what happened.

TALK IT OVER

THREE KEYS FOR FINISHERS

Quitting is an epidemic these days. Here's how quitter thinking goes: If you've made a commitment to help with a project but you're invited to something that sounds more fun, *quit*. If you're in a friendship, and you have a misunderstanding, *quit*. If that difficult class might ruin your grade point average, *quit*. If a job is boring, *quit*. If your team is having a losing season, *quit*. But here's the problem: Quitters never win; finishers do. If you want to be real in a fake world, you've got to persevere in the race of life. You've got to run that race all the way to the finish. Nothing real is accomplished—no dream is realized, no races are won—without persevering to the end and finishing.

Shout out some things you have accomplished because you had perseverance.

Let's find out from the Bible what it takes to be a finisher.

1. FINISHERS FOCUS ON THE PRIZE.

To maintain the highest level of devotion to both their training and the race itself, winning athletes focus on the prize—whether it's the gold medal, the prestige, the world record, or the residual sponsorships and endorsements! When there is a big prize at stake, a true champion will not wreck her concentration by thinking about past failures (which can be paralyzing) or past victories (which can cause carelessness).

> *Forgetting what is behind and straining toward what is ahead, I press on toward the goal to win the prize for which God has called me heavenward in Christ Jesus.* (Philippians 3:13-14)

What is the "prize" in the Christian life? What kinds of things should be taking place in a Christian's life between now and reaching the "prize"? (Think about what we've learned in this study, and then envision what God might want to do with your life.)

How can thinking about past failures make you feel like quitting? How can thinking about past victories make you feel like quitting? How can the ultimate prize motivate you to keep going even when you're discouraged, criticized, or frustrated?

2. FINISHERS GO THROUGH TRAINING.

When a rùnner prepares for a race, she lifts weights and eats properly, so that her metabolism, muscles, and body weight are all in tune to give her the greatest stamina and the fastest speed. The training we go through in the Christian life involves getting rid of the entanglements that slow us down.

> *Let us throw off everything that hinders and the sin that so easily entangles. And let us run with perseverance the race marked out for us.* (Hebrews 12:1)

Notice that there are two types of things to throw off—hindrances and sin. *Hindrances* would be things we looked at in the Quitter's Quiz that drag us down, like discouragement, criticism, and frustration. But beyond that, there is also *sin* that can keep us from running well in the spiritual race of life—in the same way that a smoker would have trouble trying to run in the Olympics. If you have a wrong relationship, a bad habit, some problem you're hiding, or a pattern of disobedience, you are sabotaging yourself and making it hard to race.

What are some of the hindrances or sins that entangle you? How do they keep you from achieving what you really want in life? How can you actually "throw them off"?

3. FINISHERS RACE TO THE END.

Stay diligent to the end of the race. If you are trying to have a daily quiet time, and you miss three days in a row, you might think, "I can't be consistent. I'm going to give up." Or, if you are going through a time in your life when you've felt far away from God, you may say, "It's too late. I've wasted so much of my life; I've blown my chance to be of any use to God now." Well, that's quitter thinking. Just because you failed once, or even several times, that doesn't mean you throw in the towel. When you feel like quitting, don't. Your perseverance will do something inside you:

> *Let perseverance finish its work so that you may be mature and complete, not lacking anything.* (James 1:4)

What happens, according to this verse, when you let perseverance finish its work? Imagine yourself "mature and complete"—what kinds of things will be different about you then, compared to the way you are now?

CHECK IN WITH YOUR MAKEOVER TEAM

From *The Quitter's Quiz*, share with your team the kinds of situations that make you most likely to quit. Go to your Makeover Journal for this week and choose your Makeover Challenge; share with your team which one you chose and why. Since this is your last week of the study, get together for a private party with your Makeover Team, and celebrate persevering through this whole study!

THE *REALLY* AMAZING RACE

MAKEOVER JOURNAL WEEK 9

CHOOSE A MAKEOVER CHALLENGE

Stop quitting and quit stopping! *Choose the Makeover Challenge corresponding with what usually makes you quit. Write about your results in your Makeover Journal or blog about it at www.headtosoulmakeover.com.*

If you are most likely to quit due to...	...try this Makeover Challenge to develop more perseverance.
Discouragement	☐ **Try again.** I will choose an area where I've failed (such as having devotions, a sports team tryout, obeying my parents, a subject in school, or kicking a habit), and I will overcome my discouragement and try again.
Criticism	☐ **Improve the quality.** I will choose one task I've grown lazy about doing (such as cleaning my room, helping with dinner, writing papers, practicing an instrument, keeping up with homework) and I will start doing it better—maybe even doing more than what is expected of me.
Frustration	☐ **Finish a project.** I will choose one unfinished project I have been avoiding because it's too big or too hard, and I will tackle it and complete it.

DATE: ______________________

Today, I showed perseverance when...

____

____

DATE: ______________________

Today, I showed perseverance when...

____

____

DATE: ______________________

Today, I showed perseverance when...

____

____

DATE: ______________________

Today, I showed perseverance when...

____

____

DATE: ______________________

Today, I showed perseverance when...

____

____

DATE: ______________________

Today, I showed perseverance when…

____

____

DATE: ______________________

Today, I showed perseverance when…

____

____

EPISODE 10

THE BIG REVEAL PARTY

CHAT ABOUT IT

Looking back at last week's Makeover Challenge, share a way you tried again to accomplish a task you'd previously failed, an area where you improved the quality of your work, or a project that you were able to finally finish. How did it feel to persevere?

TRY IT OUT

LET'S HAVE A BIG REVEAL PARTY!

Many makeover reality shows end with a Big Reveal party, where friends and family gather to see the results of all the hard work that's been done. Whether it's a room or a whole house or a hairstyle or a wardrobe, the transformation from a makeover is often stunning.

Today we're going to celebrate *your* transformation. It may not feel like you're a totally new person yet. You may feel like you've still got some work to do. Actually, the Bible tells us that there will *always* be work to do, and we won't be finished until we reach heaven. But look what it says about *who* is doing the work:

> *And I am sure that God who began the good work within you will keep right on helping you grow in his grace until his task within you is finally finished on that day when Jesus Christ returns.* (Philippians 1:6, TLB)

This Big Reveal Party is a celebration of the work that has already begun in you—the work that God has begun in you! You have partnered with God and taken some first steps, practiced new skills, thought about Bible truths, and tracked your progress in your journal. Now, it's time to celebrate the good work you have started through this study.

Enjoy the party!

P.S. Go to the online Big Reveal Party at www.headtosoulmakeover.com and sign the Real Girl Wall to commemorate your transformation.

Share Your Thoughts

With the Author: Your comments will be forwarded to the author when you send them to *zauthor@zondervan.com.*

With Zondervan: Submit your review of this book by writing to *zreview@zondervan.com.*

Free Online Resources at www.zondervan.com

Zondervan AuthorTracker: Be notified whenever your favorite authors publish new books, go on tour, or post an update about what's happening in their lives at www.zondervan.com/authortracker.

Daily Bible Verses and Devotions: Enrich your life with daily Bible verses or devotions that help you start every morning focused on God. Visit www.zondervan.com/newsletters.

Free Email Publications: Sign up for newsletters on Christian living, academic resources, church ministry, fiction, children's resources, and more. Visit www.zondervan.com/newsletters.

Zondervan Bible Search: Find and compare Bible passages in a variety of translations at www.zondervanbiblesearch.com.

Other Benefits: Register yourself to receive online benefits like coupons and special offers, or to participate in research.